HABITAT FOR HUMANITY

One Family at a Time

Twenty-Five Years of

BUILDING HOUSES AND HOPE

NOTE: HOUSE TOTALS THROUGHOUT THE TEXT ARE VALID THROUGH THE YEAR 2000

ISBN: 0-917841-99-9

© 2001 Habitat for Humanity International

1 2 3 4 5 6 7 8 9

Library of Congress Control Number: 2001 131912

A FIRST EDITIONS BOOK
produced by
SMALLWOOD & STEWART, INC.
NEW YORK CITY

Editor: MARY BETH BREWER
Designer: ALEXIS SIROC

Printed in Singapore

**Habitat for Humanity®
International**

121 Habitat Street, Americus, GA 31709

*Jesus said, "If one of you wants to be great,
he must be like the Son of Man, who did not come to be served,
but came to serve and to give His life for others."*

Matthew 20:27-28

The Bible in Today's English version; The American Bible Society, 1976

Habitat for Humanity's ultimate goal is to eliminate poverty housing and homelessness from the face of the earth by building adequate, basic housing. All of our words and actions are for the purpose of putting shelter on the hearts and minds of people in such a powerful way that poverty housing and homelessness become socially, politically, and religiously unacceptable in our nations and world.

Preface

Life's journey—from our childhood homes near Plains, Georgia, to our years in the White House, to our peacemaking efforts and humanitarian work through The Carter Center—has taught Rosalynn and me that profound experiences often come in quiet, surprising ways. Through sweat and sore muscles, for example.

Each year since 1984, we have been privileged to join thousands of other Habitat for Humanity volunteers in building houses with people who desperately need them. When others ask why we are so committed to this work, my answer is simple: "Have you ever viewed hurt replaced by hope? Have you seen fear replaced by joy? Have you had the privilege of working side-by-side with someone to build a better life?"

Human rights means not only being free from persecution...it also involves the most basic of human needs—food, clothing, and shelter. Habitat for Humanity has been building houses and hope for 25 years now, providing simple and affordable shelter for more than 500,000 people. We are thankful to have been small players in this exciting global effort.

Former U.S. President Jimmy Carter

"Habitat has opened up unprecedented opportunities for me to cross the chasm that separates those of us who are free, safe, well fed and housed, financially secure, and influential enough to shape our own destiny from our neighbors who enjoy few, if any, of these advantages."

The Crazy Idea That Works

"Everyone—all of us, every last person on God's earth—deserves decent shelter. It speaks to the most basic of human needs—our home—the soil from which all of us either blossoms or withers."

Millard Fuller

The idea for Habitat for Humanity was born at Koinonia Farm, a Christian community founded in southwest Georgia in 1942 that Millard Fuller first visited in 1965.

Clarence Jordan (right) was one of Koinonia Farm's founders. The community practiced nonviolence, welcomed all races, and shared their possessions. With Fuller, Jordan developed the concept of partnership housing.

"What the poor need is not charity but capital, not caseworkers but co-workers. And what the rich need is a wise, honorable, and just way of divesting themselves of their overabundance. The Fund for Humanity will meet both of these needs."

Clarence Jordan

IN THE PAST TWENTY-FIVE YEARS, MILLARD AND LINDA FULLER have carried Habitat for Humanity's simple yet profound message to thousands of people worldwide: that everyone, no matter where he or she lives, deserves decent housing. It is a message of partnership, between those in need and those who volunteer to help, and of inclusion, crossing religious and geographical lines. It is also a message of transformation: the power of building these homes to change the lives of everyone involved. So it is only natural that the story of Habitat itself begins with a personal transformation.

By the time Millard Fuller had turned 29, he was a millionaire. His marketing company had thrived during his years in law school. But as his finances flourished his marriage and his health fell apart. Facing these crises, the Fullers made a daring move: In 1965, they sold everything they owned and gave the money to the poor. That same year they visited Koinonia Farm, a Christian community located near Americus, Georgia. Impressed by the teachings of Koinonia's leader, Clarence Jordan, in 1968 the Fullers moved to the farm with their two young children.

It was at Koinonia that Jordan and Fuller developed the concept of "partnership housing." Those in need of homes would work side-by-side with volunteers to build simple, decent houses. The houses were to be built at cost, and the homeowners' mortgages would have no interest. These mortgage payments would be put into a revolving fund, the Fund for Humanity, which would in turn help build more homes. In 1969 the first partnership house was completed, and Bo and Emma Johnson became homeowners.

Millard Fuller took the concept of partnership housing to Africa, and in 1973 he and Linda moved with their family (now with four young children) to Zaire, today the Democratic Republic of Congo. Despite bureaucratic problems and technical difficulties, the Fullers completed more than 100 houses there. These simple cement-block structures replaced the unhealthy and unsafe mud-and-thatch houses so many Africans had to endure. Fuller's success in Zaire convinced him that the concept of partnership housing could work around the world. In 1976, the Fullers returned to the United States and, with like-minded associates, formed Habitat for Humanity International.

Fuller was well aware that, on the face of it, Habitat for Humanity was a crazy idea. Who would believe that selling low-income people secure, decent houses without profit would succeed? And how likely was it that thousands of volunteers would give up days, weeks, or months or even years to help this dream come true? But today partnership housing remains the guiding principle behind Habitat for Humanity International, which has housed more than 100,000 families worldwide. Twenty-five years of helping one family at a time build simple, decent, affordable houses is powerful testimony that Millard Fuller's vision gave birth to a crazy idea that works.

In 1982, Fuller returned to Zaire, where in 1973 he had first tested the idea of partnership housing.

People and Principles

1976 Habitat for Humanity International (HFHI) is founded in a chicken barn at Koinonia Farm by Millard Fuller along with his wife, Linda, and a small group of friends.

1977 Millard and Linda Fuller move to Americus, Georgia. Clive Rainey becomes Habitat's first volunteer.

1978 Habitat's first affiliate in the U.S. is formed in San Antonio, Texas.

1979 The San Antonio affiliate completes its first home, and Ernesto and Sylvia Torres become homeowners. The first Habitat house is built in Americus. An affiliate in Guatemala is approved, the first in the Latin America and Caribbean region.

1980 HFHI has 11 affiliates in the U.S. and 5 in 3 other nations.

🏠 **209 HFH HOUSES WORLDWIDE**

1981 HFHI celebrates its fifth anniversary. There are 14 affiliates in the U.S. and 7 internationally.

🏠 **342 HFH HOUSES WORLDWIDE**

1982 India forms HFHI's first affiliate in the Asia and the Pacific region.

◄ *"In my old house, there was no heat or air or fans. We had to carry water in from two to three blocks away because the landlord wouldn't fix the pipes."*

**Christine Harrison
Florence, South Carolina
United States**

"Wow, I don't have to be ▶ *ashamed of where I live. From this point on, it's all up."*

**Glendo Hamilton
Jacksonville, Florida
United States**

◄ A boy treats his brother to a piggyback ride outside their new Habitat house, one of nearly 300 built during the Jimmy Carter Work Project in 1999.

Maragondon, the Philippines

SIMPLE, DECENT HOUSES: Habitat houses are simple, strong, built for no profit, and have affordable, no-interest mortgages. Their design varies according to local customs and standards of living, but all meet local building and safety codes. And while they are basic enough to allow nonprofessionals to participate in their construction, they are more than adequate for meeting homeowners' needs.

"Here I'm not attacked by mosquitoes and the coldness from the holes in the walls of the other house. We're warm and protected."

Saloai Kaahwa
Kijwara, Uganda
▼

"Without Habitat we would be living day to day, as our incomes would barely cover expenses. We thank God and Habitat for this second chance and a way to stay together as a family."

Harry and Teresa Russell
Houston, Texas
United States

1983 HFHI marks its seventh anniversary with the Walk from Americus to Indianapolis, Indiana (700 miles). The third Sunday of September becomes HFHI's International Day of Prayer and Action for Human Habitat.

1984 Former U.S. President Jimmy Carter and his wife, Rosalynn, become Habitat partners and begin the first Jimmy Carter Work Project (JCWP) in New York City. Together with other Habitat volunteers, they renovate a 6-story, 19-unit apartment building.

🏠 **758 HFH HOUSES WORLDWIDE**

1985 The second annual JCWP takes place in New York City, where work is completed on the building begun in 1984.

1986 HFHI celebrates its tenth anniversary with its Walk from Americus to Kansas City, Missouri (1,000 miles). The first Canadian affiliate is approved. About 150 volunteers build a four-unit townhouse in this year's JCWP in Chicago.

1987 The Campus Chapters program, the Covenant Church program, and the Appropriate Technology department are started. U.S. Regional Centers are approved. Habitat moves to a new headquarters, entirely funded by donations. Some 235 JCWP volunteers build 14 houses in Charlotte, North Carolina.

1988 Habitat celebrates its 12th anniversary with the Walk from Portland, Maine, to Atlanta, Georgia (1,200 miles), and builds 120 houses along the way. Habitat's Global Village program and Corporate Donor department are established. At the JCWP in Philadelphia, Pennsylvania, 200 volunteers renovate a 10-unit townhouse. In Atlanta, 20 houses go up. Habitat's first South American project is completed with the dedication of 163 houses in Peru.

🏠 3,834 HFH HOUSES WORLDWIDE

1989 Hurricane Hugo strikes South Carolina and all Habitat houses in the state survive. In Milwaukee, Wisconsin, the JCWP completes six new houses and renovates eight others.

1990 The first overseas campus chapter is formed in Papua New Guinea. Bo and Emma Johnson, the first housing partners at Koinonia in Georgia pay off their mortgage. In its largest event to date, the JCWP builds 100 houses in Tijuana, Mexico, and 7 in San Diego.

1991 Habitat celebrates its 15th anniversary and builds its 10,000th house in Atlanta, Georgia. The first all-women-built house is completed in Charlotte, North Carolina. In Miami's Liberty City area, more than 400 JCWP volunteers build 14 houses and a day-care center.

Volunteers and future homeowners work together to raise a wall during the Jimmy Carter Work Project in 1998.

**Houston, Texas
United States**

Villagers put in their sweat equity placing trusses on top of a house. In this remote region, houses customarily are constructed of brick and have thatched roofs. Habitat provides mortgages that make it possible to add sturdy clay tile roofs.

Liuli, Tanzania
▼

SWEAT EQUITY: All future Habitat homeowners are required to contribute hundreds of hours of "sweat equity" building their homes or the homes of others. This not only gives them a stake in their homes, but it also helps to keep costs down. And because homeowners often work side-by-side with one another and with other Habitat volunteers, it helps foster a sense of community—something as important to Habitat as the houses themselves.

◀ Family members build their new Habitat house alongside their old thatched hut.

Bangalore, India

"It makes us all feel better ▶ *in different ways. The children aren't ashamed to invite their friends over."*

**Daphne Lewis
Americus, Georgia
United States**

◀ Future homeowners **Emmanuel Takyii** and his son, **Edward Botwe**, prepare the foundations of a Habitat house.

Assin Fosu, Ghana

1992 All of Habitat's houses in the Miami, Florida, area survive Hurricane Andrew. The Sumter County Initiative begins in Georgia with the goal of eliminating poverty housing in the county by 2000. The JCWP completes ten houses in Washington, D.C., one by an all-women crew, and ten rowhouses are rehabilitated in the Sandtown area of Baltimore, Maryland. Almost 1,000 volunteers are involved this year. HFH Alaska is approved, marking the spread of Habitat to all 50 states and the District of Columbia.

🏠 **19,032 HFH HOUSES WORLDWIDE**

1993 HFHI completes its 20,000th house during a 20-house blitz build in Americus, Georgia. India's 1,000th house is built. In Canada, the Carters are joined by 1,100 volunteers in Winnipeg, Manitoba, building 18 houses, and in Waterloo, Ontario, building 10 houses. Twelve Zambian volunteers travel to Botswana to help a new affiliate build; this is the first African cross-border work project.

1994 Habitat houses survive the devastating Los Angeles, California, earthquake and floods in Georgia. Habitat completes its 30,000th house. Former U.S. Department of Housing and Urban Development (HUD) Secretary Jack Kemp helps at Habitat's fastest house build in America: 5 hours, 57 minutes, and 13 seconds, in Pensacola, Florida. The JCWP at Cheyenne River Indian Reservation in Eagle Butte, South Dakota, builds 30 houses.

1995 Building on Faith Week becomes part of the annual Day of Prayer and Action for Human Habitat. Habitat's 40,000th house is completed. More than 1,500 volunteers from 39 states and 5 countries join the JCWP in the Watts/Willowbrook area of Los Angeles, California, where 20 houses are constructed. Builds also are held at five other sites in southern California.

1996 Habitat celebrates its 20th anniversary and dedicates its 50,000th house. U.S. President Bill Clinton honors Millard Fuller with the Presidential Medal of Freedom, the nation's highest civilian honor. Habitat conducts a 20-house blitz build in Habitat's hometown of Americus, Georgia. For the first time, the Carters build in Europe, in Vác, Hungary, alongside 500 other JCWP volunteers from 23 countries.

🏠 **51,596 HFH HOUSES WORLDWIDE**

1997 The Latin America/Caribbean Training and Resource Center is established in Costa Rica. Oprah Winfrey launches her "Build an Oprah House" project. Habitat is judged one of America's top twelve charities by *The NonProfit Times*. Appalachia is the site of the JCWP; more than 50 houses go up in Kentucky and Tennessee.

🏠 **60,404 HFH HOUSES WORLDWIDE**

1998 The 70,000th house is built. When Hurricanes Mitch and Georges attack Central America and the

"One of the greatest ▶ contributions a company can make is to support employees who choose to volunteer for Habitat." Employees from **Andersen Windows**, one of Habitat's Corporate Sponsors, after working on the 2000 Jimmy Carter Work Project in Americus, Georgia.

"Habitat conveys the very important message to people that we can all be friends," says Japanese student **Mariko Asano** of her work in the Philippines.

Retired architect **Art Hansen** now volunteers his skills and helps design and build Habitat houses, in Hawaii in winter and in Michigan in summer.
▼

VOLUNTEERS: Habitat is a grassroots movement fueled by hundreds of thousands of volunteers who join with future homeowners to build houses. Volunteers run the gamut from college students on spring break to retirees. Whether working with local affiliates or on international Global Village trips, they can build just around the corner or halfway around the world.

◀ A Bike-and-Build effort in 1997 raised money for Habitat and completed six houses.

Hoima, Uganda

"I'm a huge, huge fan of the ▶ *way Habitat works," says actress* **Susan Sarandon**, *painting in New York City. "Making movies doesn't have this kind of satisfaction, but it's the same sense of collaboration."*

Caribbean, nearly all Habitat homes survive. Millard Fuller leads an emergency campaign, raising more than US$6 million to aid victims. In Houston, Texas, 1,500 JCWP volunteers from around the world are joined by 4,500 Houstonians to build 100 houses in a week.

🏠 71,281 HFH HOUSES WORLDWIDE

1999 HFHI completes its 80,000th house. Habitat launches its 21st Century Challenge, with the goal of eliminating substandard housing in participating communities within 20 years. The JCWP in the Philippines is the largest ever, gathering together 14,000 volunteers from 32 countries. They complete 293 houses.

🏠 87,325 HFH HOUSES WORLDWIDE

2000 In Georgia, the Sumter County Initiative is achieved, eliminating the need for anyone to live in substandard housing. The JCWP builds in New York (22 houses), Georgia (35 houses), and Florida (100 houses). Habitat's 100,000th house is completed in Harlem in New York City. *Builder* magazine ranks Habitat 15th in its listing of the top 100 homebuilders in the U.S.

🏠 104,000 HFH HOUSES WORLDWIDE

2001 Habitat celebrates its 25th anniversary. It has more than 2,000 affiliates in 76 countries and has built more than 100,000 houses worldwide. The JCWP heads to the Republic of Korea.

Decent Homes, Better Lives AFRICA

SUBSTANDARD HOUSE: Traditional mud-and-thatch huts, such as this example in Ghana, are common in much of Africa. The structures are frequently cramped, unhealthy, and time-consuming to maintain. When it rains, their mud walls deteriorate, the floors turn into sludge, and water seeps through the roofs.

Thatch roofs are often home to disease-carrying insects, rodents, and snakes, and many must be replaced every few years. To harvest material for thatch, surrounding vegetation is stripped; in some areas families have to walk many miles to redo a single roof.

Five or more people may live squeezed into a **single room** 100 square feet or less in size. Typically, there is no means of sanitation.

During periods of intense rain, water erodes the **foundations of the mud walls**, sometimes causing the entire structure to collapse. **Mud walls** are also vulnerable to termites and must have constant, laborious repairs.

Doors and windows are often makeshift and inadequate. Disease and respiratory problems increase without adequate air circulation or light.

Floors are of pounded earth or cow dung and need regular maintenance.

HABITAT HOUSE: Like Habitat houses worldwide, this example in Malawi is simple and decent and provides a sound, practical, healthy environment for its inhabitants. Using locally made materials, such as roof tile and brick, provides employment and keeps the house sustainable and affordable.

Tile roofs will outlast most thatch roofs. Most people can afford a tile roof, so once Habitat has built a house, neighbors can use the roof as a model.

Vent blocks at the top of the wall allow warm air to escape, improving air circulation.

Walls are manufactured from durable, weather-resistant brick. A typical three-room house in Malawi is about 260 square feet and has its own composting toilet or pit latrine.

Windows provide ventilation and light and keep the interior of the house healthful, dry, and comfortable. A door that locks gives a family security and protects its belongings. The porch provides a sheltered entry and reflects Malawi's tradition of sitting outdoors.

Vegetation planted near the house helps prevent soil erosion. Floors are easy-to-maintain concrete.

Decent Homes, Better Lives UNITED STATES

SUBSTANDARD HOUSE: This shack in Georgia virtually defines what the U.S. Department of Housing and Urban Development classifies as substandard housing. It is estimated that 1.2 million U.S. households lack plumbing or a complete kitchen, adequate electricity, or heating, or they have serious structural or maintenance problems. Poor housing is not just unpleasant to live in; it is also dangerous, unhealthful, and expensive to maintain.

The **roof** has deteriorated, so rain leaks inside and rots the structure of the house.

Lead-based paint exposure, even in low levels, can have adverse effects on the brain and nervous systems of children. Fifty percent of housing in the United States has some lead-based paint. Asthma and other respiratory problems are also by-products of substandard housing conditions.

Broken windows and holes in the walls and the roof are invitations to insects and vermin that carry diseases.

Fires are often caused by old wiring or exposed flame heating systems. Nearly 200 children die each year from fires attributable to faulty electrical systems or heating accidents or failures; many more suffer severe burns.

Inadequate insulation diverts precious income to inflated heating bills.

HABITAT HOUSE:
Exact designs of Habitat houses vary and are modified by local codes and input from prospective homeowners. Habitat's goal is for all homes to be structurally sound and secure, safe, energy efficient, and easy to maintain. From start to finish (including basic landscaping), a typical Habitat house in the U.S. takes about 2,000 volunteer hours to build.

Concrete tile roofs, which have been used on some Habitat houses, will last several decades.

Generally, Habitat houses are built to **higher specifications** than regular homes. House plans provide for ease of mobility within the house for disabled persons.

Insulation makes the houses comfortable and easier to heat or cool. Habitat is designing energy-efficient homes that drastically cut utility bills.

New **wiring and heating** systems create a safer house. Habitat houses include modern plumbing for the kitchen, bath, and laundry areas.

Low-maintenance exterior finishes will last for decades.

The Excitement Is Building AFRICA

Habitat houses are gradually replacing the mud-and-thatch houses in the small community of Chisamba in central Zambia. A typical Habitat house in this area has one bedroom and is about 240 square feet in size, with a small veranda. In addition to building, Habitat conducts training sessions in bricklaying and roof building, which are very popular among prospective homeowners.

1. All vegetation is cleared from the land. Foundation trenches are dug for the perimeter and interior walls.

2. Stone is carried to the site for the foundation trenches. Children often help carry materials for the houses.

3. The corner blocks of the house are laid in a bed of mortar on the foundation. A string line, set level and square, marks the outside of the building. The level of the top of the corner brick is set by measuring down from this line.

4. Water is carried to the site from a nearby well to mix with cement and sand to make mortar. The area inside the foundation is built up with earth.

5. Stones are pounded into the earth to form a solid base for the floor. A plastic damp-proof course is placed on the foundation brick to stop ground moisture from wicking up the wall and supporting fungal, mold, and mildew growth, which can lead to respiratory problems.

6. The corners are built up several courses higher by the lead mason. To ensure that the walls remain plumb and level, the corners hold string lines to guide other workers laying bricks on the rest of the walls. As the walls are being built, door and window frames are set in place and fastened to the walls.

7. Window frames are sealed to the wall with mortar to keep out drafts, dust, critters, and water. Doors and window shutters are hung. When the walls reach full height, the wood roof structure is placed on the walls. Then, handmade concrete roof tiles are tied onto the wood purlins (horizontal structural roof members). Inside, a floor of cement and aggregate mix is laid.

The Excitement Is Building UNITED STATES

In keeping with the principle of building simple, decent, affordable houses, Habitat for Humanity International guidelines specify that the living space should be not more than 900 square feet for a two-bedroom house; 1,050 square feet for a three-bedroom house; and 1,150 square feet for a four-bedroom house.

1. The house site is cleared and graded. In the interests of conserving the environment and low-maintenance, some affiliates save the natural vegetation and use it for landscaping the home site.

2. Batten boards are set level at the corners and string lines are pulled as guides to mark the ground for footings. Grade stakes are set; concrete is poured and screed level to the top of the stakes. Starting at the corners, concrete blocks are laid level and plumb; string lines guide the block-laying.

3. The area under the floor is filled and compacted. Plumbing is laid in trenches and left to be connected to fixtures. Insecticide is sprayed over the ground, and then a plastic vapor barrier and wire mesh are laid on top.

4. Concrete is poured for the floor and the wire mesh is pulled up into the slab as it is screed level. In cold climates rigid insulation is laid under the concrete for energy efficiency. The slab is floated and allowed to set until it will take a smooth finish with a steel trowel.

5. After the slab has cured, wall frames are laid out and nailed together. The slab provides a convenient, flat work area. Starting with the exterior of the house, the walls are built with pre-framed window and door openings, raised, and braced to the slab.

6. Sheathing is applied to the walls to act as extra insulation and to form a drainage plane under the siding. Roof trusses are set two feet apart and braced, ready for the roof sheathing, which forms an important bracing element for the whole structure. Roof felt and shingles are laid on top. Thermal pane, insulated windows and pre-hung, weather-stripped doors are set so the house can be closed and locked.

7. Durable, weather-resistant exterior cladding is installed: soffit, fascia, and siding. Interior work begins: plumbing, heating, and electrical systems are roughed in, followed by insulation, air sealing, and drywall. Finally, the walls are painted, doors hung, kitchen cabinets installed, and flooring laid.

Uganda

Georgia, U.S.

Papua New Guinea

New Zealand

Korea

Poland

Sri Lanka

One Need, Many Solutions

The need for good, affordable housing cuts across borders and cultures. So does Habitat for Humanity, which helps people in 76 countries build decent homes. Habitat designs for simplicity and sustainability; houses are made with local materials whenever possible and can be maintained by their owners.

Although all Habitat houses share the same principles, they are adapted to meet local tastes and they employ local solutions to solve local needs. In parts of Kenya, for example, Habitat houses are made from timber treated with diesel fuel to repel termites, while log cabins in Mongolia are insulated with straw and wool. In New Mexico, houses are made from adobe; in Papua New Guinea, they are built on stilts to be flood resistant. And the blocks used to make many Habitat houses in Africa and Latin America are made of soil with a Habitat-devised technique that the community can turn into a revenue-generating business.

New York, U.S.

Fiji

Brazil

El Salvador

England

Colombia

California, U.S.

Africa and the Middle East

"Habitat helps to build a community. People get together. They build houses, but they build more than that. They build a caring community. They learn that they themselves can do something about the situation they are in. The empowerment spins off into so many other things for them."

Marcella Mukasa, Steering Committee, HFH Uganda

AFRICA AND THE MIDDLE EAST

A World of Need

The fact that Habitat for Humanity has been able to work with families to build more than 20,000 houses in Africa is remarkable, given the challenges posed by working on a continent larger than the United States, China, India, and Argentina combined. More remarkable still is the extraordinary growth of interest in Habitat at a grassroots level—in towns and villages across this vast continent.

Africa is home to nearly one billion people and a wealth of cultures and religions. The land is a rich source of gems, minerals, oil, gas, and timber, as well as some of the most celebrated wildlife and natural areas in the world. Land and land ownership play pivotal roles here: Most people live on tribal land subject to complex and often unwritten ownership rules. Furthermore, two-thirds of the population are subsistence farmers who eke out a precarious living on the little good land available (only 6 percent of the land is arable). Droughts and famines are endemic, and violent civil unrest has plagued almost every sub-Saharan nation in the past decade. All have resulted in massive internal migrations of literally millions of people. Too frequently, these refugees end up in camps or slums in large cities ill equipped to cope with the influx. At the same time, disease—malaria, river blindness, diarrhea, and tuberculosis—routinely renders adults unable to work and to feed their families. In Zimbabwe and Botswana, as many as one in four people may be infected with AIDS, an epidemic that is creating millions of orphans. Yet amidst the instability and overwhelming social and economic problems, Habitat is finding ways to create an impact, through strategic partnerships with organizations such as World Vision,

Kenya

the Lions Club, and the American Leprosy Mission, and through a strong community-based strategy.

Africa is familiar territory for Habitat. In 1973, before Habitat for Humanity International (HFHI) was born, founders Millard and Linda Fuller first brought the concept of partnership housing to the regional capital of Mbandaka in the Democratic Republic of Congo (DRC), then known as Zaire. HFHI's first overseas volunteers worked there.

That long experience has helped solidify Habitat's reputation as something much more than a mere builder of houses. It avoids the paternalistic outlook left over from colonial rule by stressing that the answers to Africa's housing problems lie within Africa—in the initiative of its people. Habitat begins work only when a community has demonstrated its commitment to helping itself by, for example, organizing an affiliate. That way, those being helped become accountable to the people who matter most—themselves. This local empowerment has been key to Habitat's success. As regional vice-president Harry Goodall explains, "A lot of times, when we explain our program to people in a village they say, 'Why do we need you?' And we say, 'You're right. You don't need us.' That's when the transformation takes place and they realize that eliminating poverty housing is something they can do."

Habitat plans to build 20,000 more houses in Africa by 2005 by working with its partners, by continuing to develop local affiliates, and by expanding into new countries. Some might consider this goal overly ambitious, but, as Jimmy Carter notes, Habitat's efforts are beginning to make a significant impact on Africa. Says the former U.S. president, "Habitat has made promises to the people of Africa, and it's been able to keep them."

A Pervasive Problem

Traditional housing in **Kenya** has dirt floors and mud walls blackened with accumulated soot and is sometimes shared with livestock. Habitat houses have concrete floors, and sturdy walls and roofs, and they often include small outside shelters for animals.

Mud-and-thatch houses, like these in **Ghana**, are common throughout Africa. Made of readily available materials, they can be practical structures, but the worst of them are cramped, unsafe, and home to disease.

Tanzania is one of the world's poorest and least urbanized countries; this young man's village is a 14-hour walk to the nearest bus route. Still, by helping start small factories to make building materials, Habitat is able to begin construction in remote regions.

In Cairo, **Egypt**, a community of families salvage garbage from dumps, then bring it to their homes where they recycle what they can and feed scraps to the pigs they keep. Children, animals, and garbage shared one room until Habitat—in conjunction with the Coptic Evangelical Organization for Social Services—began adding another level to their houses, so that families could live in more sanitary conditions, above the animals and garbage.

Kenya

Ghana

Tanzania

Egypt

A Struggle
for Survival

Uganda has suffered greatly in the last few decades from brutal political oppression. Despite a wealth of natural resources—fertile farmland, dense forests, and powerful rivers— it remains one of Africa's poorest countries. Eighty percent of its people make their living as subsistence farmers for whom survival is a constant struggle: The average life span is just 45 years, one of the lowest in Africa.

Once settled in stable, secure Habitat houses, homeowners in Uganda can develop their own small businesses and further improve their lives.

Nsinda Village, Uganda

Stronger than Bricks

Yoana Maria Mukasa was a young boy when his father brought him to the Buluba Hospital to be treated for leprosy. There he received care, was trained as a tailor, and became part of the community of sufferers. He was finally cured, but he remained a "Dead Person," a social outcast, because of his leprosy. When Mukasa learned he could become a Habitat homeowner if he made 4,000 bricks, he turned for help to the only community he really knew.

"He said he had no way to make the bricks himself," says Dr. Joseph Kawuama, deputy director of leprosy and tuberculosis programs for Uganda. "I agreed that if he could get his friends and family to help him make 2,000 bricks, I would help him get the other 2,000."

Dr. Kawuama explains that housing has become a focus of his work with leprosy patients. Even when they are cured, most of them are shunned by their villages and end up forming shanty communities around the hospitals. Dr. Kawuama sees Habitat as a way to break this cycle of dependency: "If they internalize the Habitat principles of sweat equity and the revolving fund, they discover other things they can do."

Mukasa and his friends found that they could gather materials for bricks by working together. Habitat field office director Sebastian Wukhoola cheered them on. "Those who have fingers, work with the shovels," he told them. "The rest can entertain the workers." Mukasa soon had his bricks.

Mukasa's son helped build the house, as did members of 23 families once afflicted with leprosy. And for the first time in his life, Mukasa worked with nondisabled friends—other Habitat homeowners performing their sweat equity by helping him. The 270-square-foot home has one bedroom and a sitting room. There is a veranda out front where he can wash and give special attention to his feet, which still feel the effects of leprosy. "I never thought I could have such a fine house," Mukasa says, adding that he is confident he can earn his monthly mortgage of US$3 by working as a tailor.

"Seeing Mukasa's beautiful house has made my patients want homes of their own," Dr. Kawuama says. "The best part is that Habitat didn't single out the leprosy community for help. It saw them as a part of the whole community that needed better housing."

By working with friends and neighbors to make bricks, Mukasa now has a roof over his head and a secure place to ply his trade.

Still Worlds Apart

Apartheid denied black South Africans the most basic human rights. It also forced many of them to live in squalid housing. Officially, apartheid ended in 1994, but housing remains poor for many South Africans. Urban squatter settlements called "accidental communities" of 500,000 people are common on the outskirts of cities such as Durban and Johannesburg. Typical squatter shacks are made of scrap cardboard, wood, and tin, and they have no running water, electricity, sanitation, or garbage services. Crime and violence are prevalent; cholera and dysentery are common killers. The end of apartheid opened up a host of land ownership issues that have made it difficult to build new houses. Habitat South Africa builds only in settlements where land title disputes have been resolved and where the government is providing grants for infrastructure, such as electricity, water, and sewerage.

In a country torn apart for decades by apartheid, Habitat's presence helps bring reconciliation by providing opportunities for people of all races and economic groups to work together building houses.

Durban, South Africa
All Together Now

Cresentie Mbeko, a member of the Zulu tribe, fled her home during the waning days of apartheid in the early 1990s. When she returned, she found her house a shambles, her garden a jungle of weeds. "We had stayed in the hills because the fighters were destroying everything," she says. "When I came back I had to fix a small house because I had my children—three boys and a girl—to care for. I had to get them inside."

A widow surrounded by other widows, Mbeko never stopped dreaming of a better future, one that included decent housing. When she found work as a domestic servant, her employer provided shelter. But Mbeko was determined to return to her land. "My madam asked, 'Do you really want to build a house?' When I said yes, she helped me get some windows and a door." Mbeko was able to build a temporary shelter in 1994 and to prepare her garden.

Then she learned about Habitat. "I heard I would need to raise [US]$150 for a deposit. How could I do that?" She joined forces with three other women to raise enough money for all of them to become Habitat homeowners. "We are old women, but together we are strong, so we said, 'First we will get the money for one house,'" Mbeko says. "We went to the factories to get scraps, we did crochet, and when we got the money from that we got seeds and planted beans, bananas, potatoes, carrots, and beetroot to sell. That way we got the money for the first house, and they chose me to receive it. Then in the same way we got the money for Agnes and next for Dora and so on." All of the women's houses were started in January 2000 when a Global Village team came to Durban, and all of them were finished in April.

Empowered by the security and stability that come from having a house of her own, Mbeko has turned her attention to improving her community. She completed a marketing course, found a donor to contribute sewing machines to her fledgling women's cooperative, and set up a sewing shop in a local school. "We took scraps others threw away and made uniforms from them," she says. "It's a community project run by women. Most of us are widows, so we must make it happen ourselves."

Raising the deposit for this Habitat house took community effort for Cresentie Mbeko. Now that she has her own home, she is building a small business with her women's cooperative. Her grandchildren enjoy playing outside.

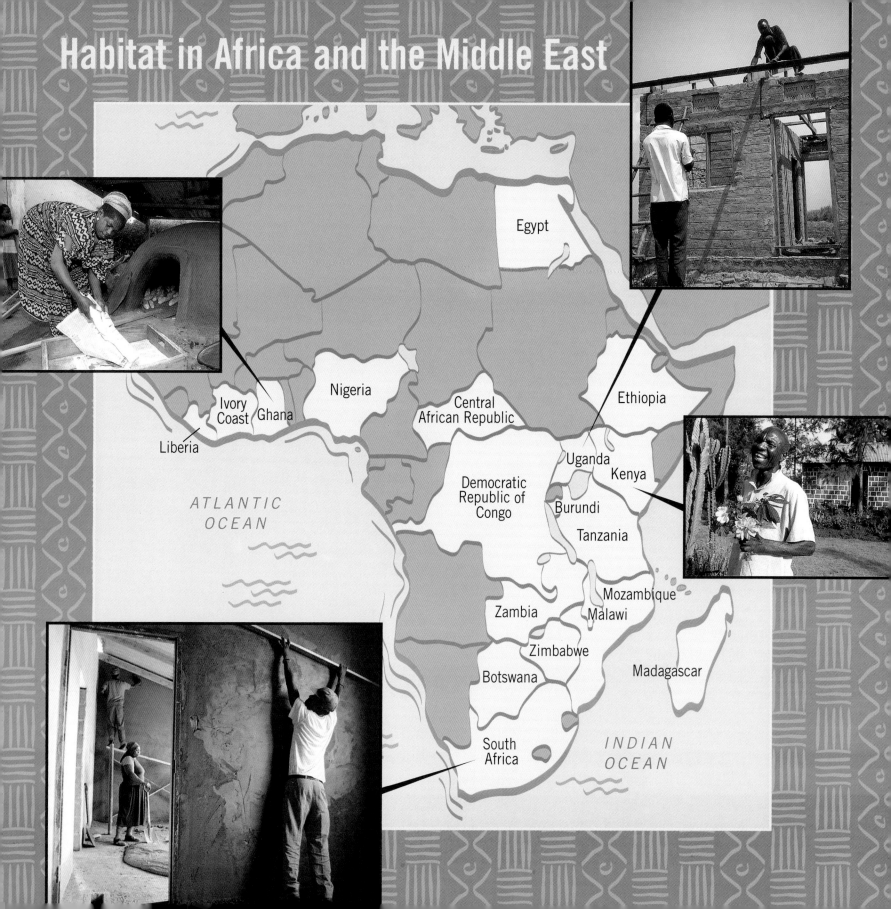

Habitat in Africa and the Middle East

Egypt

Nigeria

Central African Republic

Ethiopia

Ivory Coast Ghana

Liberia

Uganda

Kenya

ATLANTIC OCEAN

Democratic Republic of Congo

Burundi

Tanzania

Mozambique

Zambia

Malawi

Zimbabwe

Madagascar

Botswana

South Africa

INDIAN OCEAN

Botswana

Three-quarters of Botswana is covered by the Kalahari Desert, so most residents live in the scrubby plains and crowded cities of the eastern part of the country. Since starting work in 1992, Habitat Botswana has built 634 houses, primarily in rural areas. A typical concrete-block structure includes three rooms with a tile roof and a latrine or indoor toilet.

HABITAT FACT: Working with the Lions Club, Habitat is building houses for the disabled.

Burundi

Habitat began its program in 1987 with 35 houses but was forced to leave in 1993 when violence between Tutsis and Hutus killed some 150,000 people. In 1998, Habitat teamed with World Vision to build more than 800 houses in 18 months. Habitat has built nearly 1,000 houses in Burundi.

HABITAT FACT: Habitat's new homeowners include teenage orphans of the civil war.

Central African Republic

Most people of the Central African Republic (CAR) are subsistence farmers or loggers. Since entering CAR in 1991, Habitat has built more than 438 houses in 15 villages. CAR Habitat is also helping a large community of people disabled by leprosy to build houses in northern Congo.

Ivory Coast

HABITAT FACT: The monthly mortgage on a CAR Habitat house is US$8; average daily income is US$1.

Democratic Republic of Congo

Formerly known as Zaire, the Democratic Republic of Congo (DRC) is one of the world's neediest countries. Almost one-third of its people do not live to age 40. Habitat started work here in 1976 and has built an average of 95 houses a year—nearly 2,400 in all.

HABITAT FACT: All of the 33 villages on the shore of Lake Ntomba are building Habitat houses.

Egypt

Seventy-five percent of Egypt is desert, which means that most of its 65 million people live in a narrow corridor along the Nile River; estimates suggest that a quarter of the population lives in substandard housing. Since starting work in Egypt in 1990,

Habitat and its Egyptian counter-parts, including the Coptic Evangelical Organization for Social Services, have enabled 1,700 homeowners to build or renovate in eight diverse communities. The mortgage repayment rate for Habitat's sustainable-credit fund is 96 percent.

HABITAT FACT: Habitat partners conserve land by encouraging vertical construction, such as the seven-story apartment buildings in Port Said.

Ethiopia

Most private land ownership is forbidden in Ethiopia, the only African country that was not colonized by a European power. Recently, a costly border war with Eritrea and a long drought have threatened a famine. Habitat started work here in 1990 in the capital, Addis Ababa, where 80 percent of the population either is homeless or lives in sub-standard housing; Habitat has built nearly 100 houses.

HABITAT FACT: Habitat has advised UNICEF on its renovation of a shelter for street children in Addis Ababa.

Ghana

Many Ghanaians inhabit sub-standard communal housing that shelters as many as 40 members of an extended family. Active in Ghana since 1987, Habitat has helped families build more than 2,042 houses in 24 communities for about US$1,000 each.

HABITAT FACT: Ghana won Habitat Africa's 2000 Best Program award for its building, mortgage repayment, and grassroots affiliate growth.

Ivory Coast

Among the world's leading exporters of coffee, cocoa beans, and palm oil, Ivory Coast is one of the most prosperous of the West African states and has historically enjoyed political stability. This changed in 1999, when a military coup—the first in the country's history—overthrew the government.

HABITAT FACT: Habitat is in the process of developing 12 new affiliates, and families have raised money and begun to make blocks for their houses.

Kenya

Three-fourths of Kenya's 30 million people are farmers, but

Uganda

only 7 percent of the nation's land is arable, and a vast amount of that is reserved for national parks and wildlife preserves. Droughts have led to the over-harvesting of vegetation, which has led in turn to a shortage of materials for building traditional mud-and-stick huts. Since entering Kenya in 1982, Habitat and its affiliates have built more than 1,057 houses. Kenya now builds 100 houses a year but plans to increase activity to 1,000 a year by 2004.

HABITAT FACT: Kenyan law grants title to property to those who have occupied it for two years.

Liberia

Liberia has had a troubled history. A civil war from 1989 to 1996 destroyed much of its economy, especially the infrastructure in and around the capital, Monrovia. More than 60,000 families either have been displaced or are living in very poor housing conditions as a result of the fighting. Many business people fled the country, taking capital and expertise with them. Today, the country is slowly rebuilding its social, political, and economic fabric. Habitat set

Uganda

South Africa

up a national office in 2000 and has identified 32 communities in Bong, Bomi, Margibi, and Monserado counties where families want to build houses.

HABITAT FACT: Habitat Liberia hopes to build 60 houses in 2001.

Madagascar

The world's fourth-largest island, Madagascar suffers from severe deforestation and erosion. It has one of the world's fastest growing populations (3 percent annually). Habitat and its three affiliates have built six houses since entering the country in 1999.

HABITAT FACT: Habitat plans to build 80 houses on a 2.5-acre plot in the capital, Antananarivo.

Malawi

Since entering Malawi in 1985, Habitat has built more than 4,800 sturdy brick houses, more than in any other African country. The need is great: 80 percent of residents live in rural areas,

where dirt-floored shelters with thatched roofs can offer more health risks than protection. One of the most significant challenges Habitat faces in Malawi is that people have very little income with which to pay a mortgage.

HABITAT FACT: When a family applies for a Habitat home in rural Malawi, it must have the local chief's confirmation that the village or clan owns the land it wants to build on.

Mozambique

Mozambique was a Portuguese colony for almost five centuries. That ended in 1975, but the country's development has since been hindered by economic dependence on South Africa, a large external debt, severe drought, and a prolonged civil war. Recent flooding has displaced more than 1.2 million people and devastated the economy.

HABITAT FACT: Habitat entered the country in 2000. Flooding has delayed start-up work.

Nigeria

After nearly two decades of military rule, Nigeria adopted a new constitution in 1999 and completed a peaceful transition to a civilian government. The country now faces the daunting task of rebuilding a petroleum-based economy and resolving long-standing ethnic and religious tensions between northern Muslims and southern Christians.

Habitat briefly entered Nigeria in the early 1990s but left when social instability put an end to its initiatives. Habitat has established a new national office in the capital, Abuja, and hopes to begin building houses with families by January 2002.

HABITAT FACT: This country of 120 million has more people living in poverty than any other country in Africa.

Malawi

South Africa

South Africa boasts a world-class economy, but only one in seven residents enjoys a high standard of living. Most live in poor townships surrounding large cities or urban squatter settlements. Since the collapse of apartheid in 1994, one of the thorniest issues South Africa has faced is land ownership, a debacle that has paralyzed house building in some

Tanzania

black townships. Still, Habitat has built some 500 houses in South Africa since 1987, with help from groups ranging from a women's cooperative to members of the Zulu tribe.

Uganda

HABITAT FACT: Habitat's Africa and the Middle East Area Office was moved from HFHI headquarters in Americus, Georgia, to Pretoria, South Africa, in 1998 as part of a decentralization initiative.

Tanzania

Home to both Mount Kilimanjaro and Lake Victoria, Tanzania is rich in natural beauty. Yet there are so few roads that Habitat staff and volunteers rely on missionary aviators to fly into remote villages. In times of severe drought or flooding, food shortages make it difficult for Habitat families to pay their mortgages, because their crops are their only currency. Nevertheless, since entering Tanzania in 1985, Habitat has built more than 1,700 houses at an average price of US$2,500.

HABITAT FACT: In 1999, Tanzania held a highly successful First Ladies Build led by Mama Anna Mkapa, the first lady of Tanzania, in which 100 women built 20 homes.

Uganda

Habitat came to Uganda, one of the world's poorest nations, in 1982 and built 26 houses before being forced out by political turmoil. It returned three years later and resumed building in 1987. Within three years, nearly 400 houses had been built. It

has six active affiliates and has completed some 2,250 houses. Support from women's groups and First Lady Janet Museveni, as well as from a national youth program, has increased local participation in Habitat.

HABITAT FACT: The Masindi affiliate has built more than 100 houses that female title holders will be able to pass on to their heirs, a dramatic departure from local custom.

Zambia

Landlocked Zambia is a high plateau covered with thick forests and many rivers, including the mighty Zambezi. It depends on a single industry—copper mining— for 80 percent of its foreign currency. Habitat came to Zambia in 1985 and built more than 500 houses in a remote fishing village. Habitat has struggled to expand the program as deflated copper prices, drought, and food shortages have created an unsettled economy. Working with Habitat's eight affiliates, Zambian families have built more than 793 houses.

HABITAT FACT: As in many other African countries, monthly mortgage payments are calculated according to the price of a bag of cement.

Zimbabwe

Habitat has built more than 355 houses since beginning its Zimbabwe program in 1996, an impressive effort considering the country's political changes and economic crises. Zimbabwe endured a 70 percent rate of inflation in 2000; half of the work force was unemployed; and the tobacco industry, which accounts for one-fifth of the economy, was threatened by conflict over white-owned farms. (Whites make up less than 1 percent of the population but own 70 percent of Zimbabwe's land.) Still, Habitat families exceeded year 2000 construction targets of 130 houses and maintain very high mortgage repayment rates.

HABITAT FACT: More than 160 Habitat houses have been built on government-offered homesteads.

Kenya

Asia and
the Pacific

"When you give a family an opportunity to live with dignity, then they can piece a better life together. When they have a home, they have a stake in society.....
It's part of the process of making them responsible citizens."

Anthony Ng, Chairman of the Board, HFH Philippines
President, Amkor Technology Philippines

Korea

Nepal

India

ASIA AND THE PACIFIC
Complex Challenges

Two-thirds of the world's more than six billion people live in Asia and the Pacific, and their numbers continue to grow at a phenomenal pace. This vast region, encompassing the two most populous countries, China and India, and the far-flung tiny islands of the South Pacific, is a complex and often unsettled mix of cultures, ethnicities, and religions. It is home to the largest Hindu, Muslim, and Buddhist countries and to some of the world's poorest and richest nations.

Although much of Asia/Pacific shared in the global economic growth of the 1990s, one-third of its residents live in substandard housing—or no housing at all. Some of the region's most important cities are home to countless thousands of families crowded into shacks with no water or sanitary services. In fact, Asia's cities are exploding: By 2020, 50 percent of the people in Asia and 72 percent of those in the South Pacific will live in urban areas where jobs may be more plentiful but land is scarce and expensive—a major challenge to building low-income housing.

India

One of the keys to operating successfully in such a diverse region is finding innovative ways to solve problems. Habitat started a "Save and Build" program in Sri Lanka and poverty-stricken Bangladesh, for example, in which those who can save enough money for three bags of cement become eligible for HFHI's two-for-one matching grant. This allows people to replace dirt floors with permanent ones, thus reducing the incidence of disease. Families add better roofs, doors, windows, and latrines as they raise more money. For generations, tea pickers in Hatton, Sri Lanka, have

Thailand

lived in near indentured servitude. That is changing as Habitat has convinced plantation companies to donate land for houses. By early 2001, 100 houses were completed or near completion. In South Kerala, India, Habitat has partnered with Cheru Resmi Centre to create a savings plan for local fishermen so they can afford to replace the straw huts that are vulnerable to annual floods and cyclones with more permanent Habitat houses.

Natural disasters have a significant impact on housing issues throughout Asia: Frequent floods, earthquakes, and typhoons wreak havoc with shelters of all kinds, whether flimsy or sturdy. In 1991, the eruption of Mount Pinatubo in the Philippines displaced more than one million people; cyclones in Bangladesh leave tens of thousands homeless each year; and the most devastating earthquake in Indian history hit Gujarat in 2001, leaving a trail of destruction over a wide area and an estimated 600,000 people homeless.

Habitat faces issues other than natural disasters here. More than 700,000 Sri Lankans have been left homeless in the wake of 15 years of ethnic warfare between the Tamils and the Sinhalese. Habitat volunteers have worked in Sri Lanka to build "bridges" as well as houses by bringing together families from the warring factions for construction projects.

Habitat plans to build 5,000 houses annually in the region, teaming up when possible with like-minded organizations such as World Concern and World Vision. These groups provide services other than home-building, making it easier for potential homeowners to acquire and prepare land for housing and arrange for electric, water, and sewer hookups. Global partners will also play a role in Habitat's entry into countries such as Mongolia, China, and Vietnam, which have only recently opened their doors to Western aid groups.

A Basic Need

Residents of the Polonnaruwa district of southern **Sri Lanka** work in rice paddies and live in rented mud-and-thatch houses. Habitat has brought home-ownership within their reach through an innovative "Building in Stages" program that enables local people to construct small structures and enlarge them over time, a process that builds hope as well as communities.

Although Habitat works in both urban and rural **New Zealand**, the challenges it faces are greater in the countryside because of a lack of infrastructure for water, electricity, and sewerage. Still, Habitat is working with Maori groups in both the Far North and East Cape districts of the North Island to replace substandard housing with safe, modern dwellings.

The world's most densely populated country, **Bangladesh** is its wettest as well. Seventy percent of the country is under water for most of the year. Thousands of homes are destroyed every monsoon season, depriving people of a way to make an income—and to pay for shelter. But Habitat has created micro-credit programs to ensure potential homeowners regular cash flow and is developing designs for flood-resistant houses.

Sri Lanka

New Zealand

Bangladesh

A City in Crisis

Nothing depicts the poverty in the Philippines more starkly than the slums of Manila, one of the most densely populated cities in the world and one that suffers all of the pains of intense urbanization: epidemics, crime, air pollution, horrendous traffic and chronic housing shortages. Some ten million people—more than 12 percent of all Filipinos—live in the sprawling National Capital Region; one million of them live in acute poverty. The Philippine government has said that permanent housing is its citizens' single greatest need.

Most squatters in Manila pay as much or more in rent each month as local Habitat homeowners pay in mortgage.

The tremendous pressure for shelter forces families to seek refuge in makeshift shantytowns along Manila's railroads, where they live under threat of eviction. Some even build along Metro Manila's waterways, and when typhoons hit, as they frequently do, desperate residents are once again sent scrambling for shelter. Manila's poorest people live on top of the city's massive garbage dumps and survive by picking through trash for scraps to sell or to eat.

Maragondon, the Philippines
Freedom from Fear

Virginia Ramos lived in fear. Literally. She was afraid to go to sleep, afraid that the weak, leaky walls of her family's old shack would finally give way and collapse on her, her husband, Renato, and their six children.

The flimsy one-room shanty was made even more unstable by the high winds and heavy rains that frequently tear across the Philippines. Big cracks and even bigger holes shot through its bamboo walls, and when the storms came, the vulnerable shelter afforded no safety.

Even so, the Ramos family was luckier than most of the 4.2 million people who live below the poverty level on this tropical archipelago. Most people have little hope of acquiring decent shelter. Unemployment in the Philippines hovers around 10 percent; the average income for a family of six is less than US$100 a month. One-third of Filipinos live below the poverty line, and for many, eviction is a constant threat. But the Ramoses' shack was built on family land, so they didn't have to worry about being evicted.

The Ramos family's situation changed dramatically during Habitat for Humanity's 1999 Jimmy Carter Work Project. They were one of nearly 300 Filipino families chosen to build their own houses in six locations in a single week, with the help of more than 14,000 volunteers from around the world.

The Ramoses' new three-room house—made of concrete blocks, steel-reinforced concrete floors, and a metal roof with hurricane straps—offers electricity, a water-seal toilet, and a kitchen sink with running water. The 300-square-foot house has two partitioned sleeping areas, and Virginia has room out back for a small garden in which she grows vegetables to feed her family. While Renato's income as a farmer and a *barangay* captain (a sort of village chief) is as erratic as it is meager, it's enough to pay their modest mortgage.

"It makes me cry to think that we are here," says Virginia. "To those who are still living in poverty housing, I say they should keep praying and not lose hope. I am living testimony that there is hope."

And that hope can overcome fear.

Perhaps the greatest achievement of the 1999 Jimmy Carter Work Project was a renewal of the Filipino tradition of *bayanihan*—a spirit of working together—that built the Ramos family and 292 other families safe, sturdy houses.

A Cry for Help

Bangalore, India's seventh-largest city, was once known as "the Garden City" because of its mild southern climate and sprawling plantings of flowers. It is now one of India's high-tech centers, but age-old problems persist in the *jhuggi bastis*, or slums, that ring its outskirts. Many people lack the funds to live in anything more than a mud hut with a thatched roof, scant protection from the monsoon rains and cyclones that lash the country each summer.

Bangalore HFH works with widows because of the economic and social isolation the women face.

Until as recently as 1980, many of Bangalore's granite-quarry workers—men and women—were kept in overcrowded company housing as bonded laborers, forced to work 9- to 12-hour days. They are now paid for this arduous labor, and many of them can go home to a Habitat house that provides decent shelter and comfort.

Bangalore, India
Dignity and Independence

Just 23 years old when her husband died in 1992, Venkatalakshmiamma faced a life common to widows in India, particularly among the poorer classes—one of perpetual mourning and social isolation, with little chance of remarriage. There was also the possibility that she would lose her meager assets to her husband's family. But her determination to keep her family together, along with a big boost from Habitat for Humanity, helped save her from a life of social and economic deprivation.

After her husband died, Venkatalakshmiamma discovered that without his income she ran the risk of falling into debt and that the land she counted on had been sold. With three young children to raise, and with only her income from a factory job, she could no longer pay her rent. In desperation, she was forced to place her two older children with her sister, keeping only her youngest son, a toddler, with her.

But hope dawned a year later when she heard that Habitat was to begin a project in Bangalore. She borrowed money from relatives and regained the title to her husband's land. Then she applied for a Habitat house and began building sweat equity, all the while holding down her full-time job. A year later, she and her children moved into their new Habitat house, where the monthly mortgage payment is half of what her previous rent had been. With a bedroom, a kitchen, a living room and a toilet, her house fits in with the homes in her working-class neighborhood.

But Habitat helped Venkatalakshmiamma earn much more than a house. She now has her independence and a newfound sense of dignity. She still struggles financially, but she is buoyed by her religious faith, growing self-confidence, and optimism for her children's future. In a country where the illiteracy rate for women is 25 percent higher than that for men, and where many people educate only one son, it fills Venkatalakshmiamma with pride to know that her children are learning to read English in school. She knows that her country is modernizing and that literacy is almost as essential to their survival as food, water—and shelter.

Habitat's new houses in Bangalore replace flimsy old structures with sturdy dwellings made of stones and concrete blocks. Habitat's plans for the low-cost houses are widely used by other housing authorities in Bangalore.

Habitat in Asia and the Pacific

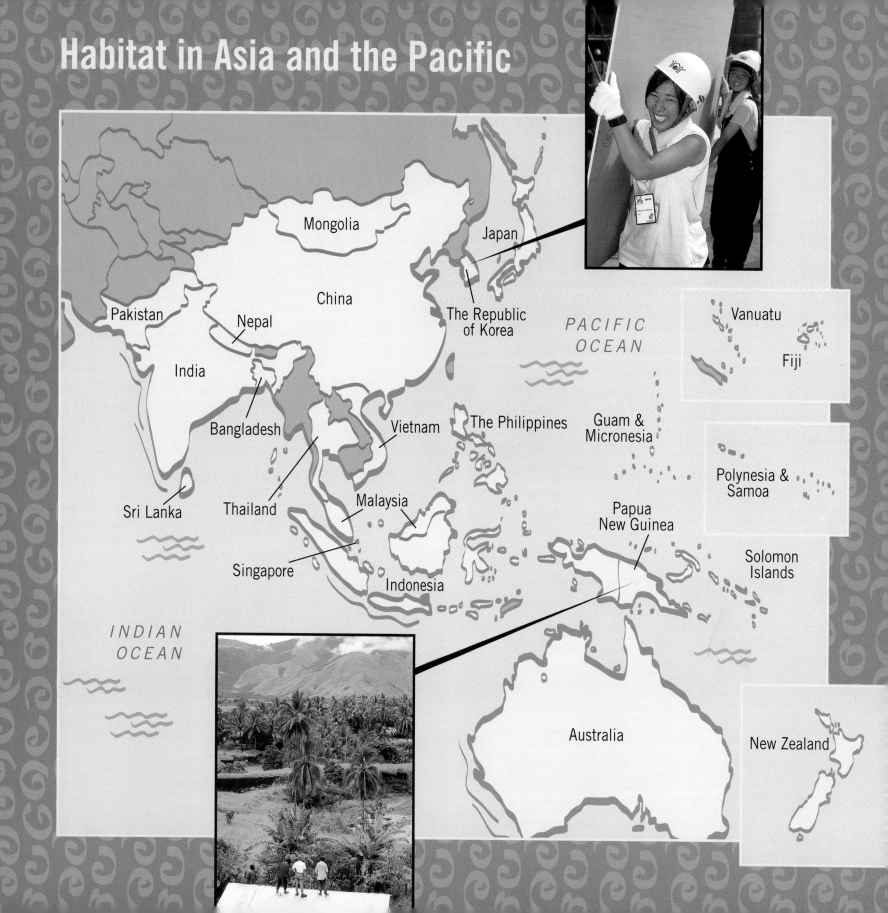

Mongolia

Japan

China

The Republic
of Korea

Pakistan

Nepal

India

*PACIFIC
OCEAN*

Vanuatu

Fiji

Bangladesh

Vietnam

The Philippines

Guam &
Micronesia

Polynesia &
Samoa

Sri Lanka

Thailand

Malaysia

Papua
New Guinea

Solomon
Islands

Singapore

Indonesia

*INDIAN
OCEAN*

Australia

New Zealand

Nepal

Australia

Habitat came here in 1988. Despite the country's relatively high standard of living, nearly 500,000 families live in housing-related poverty and over 100,000 families are homeless/transitional. The biggest obstacle is acquiring land in urban areas of the south-east, where 85 percent of Australians live. In recent years, land and construction costs have soared. As a result, Habitat also buys and renovates houses. Thanks to affiliates working in the Sydney area, 28 Australian families own Habitat homes.

HABITAT FACT: Habitat Australia has a "house for a house" policy. For every house built in Australia, an affiliate is encouraged to raise money to build a house for a family in a developing neighbor country.

Bangladesh

Floods and cyclones devastate this low-lying country. Most people are subsistence farmers who live in mud houses or shanties which

Bangladesh

are periodically swept away in floods. Poverty is acute. Many families are unable to earn and save enough money for even the most basic Habitat house. In 1999, Habitat began working in Mymensingh with families involved in a micro-savings program that fosters group savings. By 2001, more than 35 houses had been built.

HABITAT FACT: Habitat is working with engineers and architects to design a flood-resistant inexpensive, house built with indigenous, affordable materials. Currently, most houses use concrete, which is too expensive for many families.

China

In 2000, Habitat entered this country of 1.3 billion people, heading first to Yunnan Province in the remote mountains of southwestern China. The government estimates that more than 48 million Chinese still live in poverty and in inadequate housing.

Fiji

These South Pacific islands have a history of ethnic tension. In 1992, Habitat brought together families in need from both sides of the conflict to build homes on Viti Levu, Fiji's main island. Today, Habitat builds houses throughout the country. Chief among Habitat's challenges have been the zoning laws that make it impossible for certain ethnic groups to own land. In a testimony to their success, Fijian families

have built more than 439 Habitat houses, and they continued to work even when unrest in 2000 forced Habitat to move its regional offices to Australia.

HABITAT FACT: Habitat serves as an advisor to the Fijian government's Housing Ministry, which attaches copies of Habitat house plans to new land titles issued to the poor.

Guam and Micronesia

In 1996, when Habitat opened its program on Guam, it was the first self-help, low-income house-builder in the U.S territory, which lies in both an earthquake zone and Typhoon belt. The lofty price of land and imported building materials, plus stringent building codes, make housing costs here among the highest in the world (US$100,000 or more, plus expensive land plots). In 1998, Habitat built its first house—a three-bedroom concrete structure for an eight-member family. By early 2001, it had built two more and three were under construction.

HABITAT FACT: On Guam, houses must be built with concrete slab foundations and with steel-reinforced walls and roofs to withstand earthquakes

and high winds. Using alternative designs, Habitat hopes to reduce costs by as much as 65 percent.

India

India was the first Asian country Habitat entered, and it holds the record for the most houses built in the region—more than 6,000. But that's only a fraction of the housing needed here. Despite India's recent economic growth, it still has more than 100 million substandard houses. Habitat is most active in southern and central India, building houses with Hindus, Muslims, Christians, and people of other faiths.

HABITAT FACT: Following the 2001 earthquake in Gujarat, Habitat has pledged to rebuild thousands of homes. The new homes will be made with durable materials and earthquake-resistant building techniques.

Indonesia

Culturally diverse Indonesia is the fourth most populous country in the world. Most people are crammed into the island of Java, which makes up just 7 percent of the country's land area. This creates severe housing needs, exacerbated by economic and political instability and by ethnic and religious conflict. Since 1991, Habitat has built more than 65 houses.

HABITAT FACT: With the high cost of land, renovation is a successful way to obtain affordable housing.

Japan

Habitat began its work in Japan in 1997 through the local initiative of university students. Its first campus chapter was established at Kwansei Gakuin in Kobe. The main focus of campus groups is involvement in short-term mission experiences as well as raising awareness about the right to decent housing.

Fiji

HABITAT FACT: Habitat doesn't build houses in Japan but taps into one of the country's greatest resources: its youth. An estimated 25,000 young people have been involved.

Malaysia

In 1998, Habitat entered Malaysia, a multiethnic, rapidly developing country. Here land and housing regulations are complex, property is expensive, and many Malaysians lack the security of a home. Habitat works in Kuching, a city of 450,000 on the northern part of the island of Borneo. In 1999, Malaysia's first Habitat house was built—totally funded by local donations.

HABITAT FACT: Among the more than 100 volunteers participating in a recent build were members of the Malaysian Army and Navy.

Mongolia

Mongolia is the fifth-largest country in Asia, and a fledgling democracy after 66 years of a communist system ended in 1990. In rural areas, many people live in shacks without running water that are uninhabitable in the bitter-cold winters. Other Mongolians still prefer *gers*, their traditional round felt tents. Habitat entered Mongolia in 2000 and built two houses before winter. It is gearing up for summer-long building in 2001 with Global Village teams.

HABITAT FACT: Habitat houses face average winter temperatures of -13°F (-25°C) for much of the year.

Nepal

Nepal has some of the most acute housing needs in Asia. Almost half of its three million dwellings are temporary, and most have one room, which houses a family plus livestock. While land is privately owned, there are no

New Zealand

bank loans available for the poor to build houses. In its first three years in the country, Habitat built more than 225 houses.

HABITAT FACT: Habitat Nepal is one of the fastest growing programs in Asia, gaining momentum after democratic reforms focused government attention on poverty housing.

New Zealand

Habitat entered New Zealand in 1993, and found many people in urgent need. An estimated 15,000 families are living in substandard housing. Many are the indigenous Maori people living in rural areas and Pacific Islanders who are ill equipped to respond to rapid change. Habitat now has 20 affiliates and through early 2001 had built over 100 houses with New Zealanders.

HABITAT FACT: In 1999, in Auckland Habitat volunteers built the world's fastest Habitat house in 3 hours, 44 minutes, and 59 seconds—a four-bedroom house complete with curtains, a mailbox, and a new lawn.

Pakistan

In a pilot program in the 1990s, Habitat built 20 houses. Today there is no active program here. However, Habitat is hoping to restart the program.

Papua New Guinea

The island nation of Papua New Guinea is rural, and most of its five million people live in traditional bush houses, which cannot weather cyclones and must be reconstructed every four years. As a result, bamboo, timber, and vegetation are becoming scarce, resulting in erosion and a loss of soil productivity. Habitat came to Papua New Guinea in 1983 and has built more than 950 houses.

HABITAT FACT: Papua New Guinea's tropical rainforest is threatened with overharvesting by commercial logging and overuse. Habitat plants two trees for every one harvested for its builds.

The Philippines

Habitat entered the Philippines in 1986. Most Filipino families have neither the capital nor the credit to buy a simple house with a leak-proof roof to protect them from torrential monsoon rains. After building more than 3,800 houses here, Habitat hopes to soon have an affiliate in every one of the nation's 79 provinces.

HABITAT FACT: The working poor want to stay in cities where the jobs are, but urban land prices rival those in the most expensive cities in the United States.

Polynesia and Samoa

Habitat's program in Samoa is new, beginning in 2000.

The Republic of Korea

Korea is one of the Pacific Rim's newly industrialized economies. More than 80 percent of the people live in cities, where much of the housing is multi-level to maximize land use. Due to high land costs and stiff financing hurdles, approximately 22,000 low-income South Korean families cannot afford to buy a home. With land donated by a Christian communal village and money from private donors, the first houses were built in Uijongbu. Since 1995, Habitat has built more than 87 housing units.

HABITAT FACT: In 2000, a Korean blitz build called Miracle across the River Build raised US$1.5 million and brought together 1,500 volunteers to build 34 housing units in a single week.

Singapore

Because poverty housing is not a problem in Singapore Habitat for

Papua New Guinea

Humanity does not have a building program here, but it does have a presence. Funds are raised for building houses elsewhere, and volunteers are recruited from churches, businesses, and schools to help build in other countries.

Solomon Islands

Habitat came to the Solomon Islands in 1986. Since then, Habitat has struggled to build a sustainable program against a backdrop of diverse island cultures, ethnic tensions, and a rapidly growing population. The economy is one of the least developed in the South Pacific. Throughout the islands, housing is temporary, electricity unavailable (or erratic), safe drinking water insufficient, and sanitation inadequate. Malaria is a constant threat. Habitat has built more than 25 houses on the islands.

HABITAT FACT: Habitat work has begun again after temporarily being suspended because of ethnic tensions on the island of Guadalcanal and elsewhere.

Sri Lanka

Fifteen years of ethnic fighting have devastated Sri Lanka's economy and created 700,000 refugees. Most islanders who work as agricultural laborers for wealthy landowners are themselves landless and occupy mud huts in small villages. Habitat came to the island in 1994 and began working in the western and

Sri Lanka

central parts of the country. It has built more than 1,000 houses.

HABITAT FACT: Tamil volunteers helped Sinhalese tea pickers in Hatton finish building Habitat houses on land donated by the tea estates, breaking generations of poverty for workers and their families.

Thailand

Economic changes have encouraged thousands of rural poor to migrate to cities hoping to find work. Many people pay high rents to live in overcrowded slums. Habitat was invited to Thailand in 1998 to focus on housing needs in Udon Thani, a provincial center in the northeast, and other urban areas such as Chiang Mai. Since land is expensive and title issues complex, Habitat currently targets families who already own a plot of land or who have arranged long-term lease-to-buy contracts.

HABITAT FACT: Habitat's Asia/Pacific Area Office was moved from HFHI headquarters in Americus, Georgia, to Bangkok in 1998 as part of a decentralization initiative.

Vanuatu

Habitat began its program on the island of Vanuatu, in the Coral Sea, in 2000. It is a rural island covered by dense forests with narrow coastal strips of land devoted to farming. Houses will have reinforced concrete walls to withstand typhoon-force winds.

HABITAT FACT: By the end of 2001, Habitat will be prepared to host two-week builds here.

Vietnam

Habitat entered Vietnam in 2000 and began a strategic partnership with World Concern Development Organization to lay the groundwork for building homes in the city of Danang. Here 21,000 families live in substandard housing. Habitat hopes to start a demonstration house build in the fall of 2001.

HABITAT FACT: Habitat's efforts will be Vietnam's first large-scale, low-cost housing focused on poor families, with a goal of creating a sustainable building program.

"We all know that the housing needs in this country are tremendous, but Habitat offers more than a house—it can kindle people's determination and faith that life can be changed."

Jerzy Buzek, Prime Minister, Poland

Poland

Hungary

Portugal

EUROPE AND THE COMMONWEALTH OF INDEPENDENT STATES

A Time of Transition

For a continent on which families often live and work in the same communities and even inhabit the same home for generations, the recent pace of change in Europe and the republics of the former Soviet Union (known collectively as the Commonwealth of Independent States, or CIS) has been extraordinary. Some of that change has come about as a result of political moves, some as a result of economic dictates. Since starting work in Europe in 1992, Habitat for Humanity International has been a quiet, gentle presence helping those most affected by the social upheaval and those left behind in the economic changes to find decent shelter.

The collapse of the regimes that ruled eastern Europe for the second half of the last century was a triumph for personal freedom, but it also created a variety of very real problems. Without state support, residents of those countries—Armenia, Hungary, Poland, and Romania, for example—must now provide for themselves the necessities that their governments formerly furnished.

Necessities like housing. During communist rule, the state guaranteed shelter for everyone. But with the sudden change to market economies, the certainty of housing disappeared. When Habitat began its Romanian program in 1996 in the small community of Beius, there were 4,500 families in a 12-mile radius who needed housing. In nearby Arad, 7,000 were on a waiting list for homes; only 200 could be accommodated.

Other problems in the new democracies also have an impact on housing. Unemployment is high (20 percent in Armenia, for example) and income is low. Land title issues are often byzantine because property that belonged

England

Romania

to the state often reverted to the former owners—if they could be found. And ethnic conflicts that the communists repressed with force roared back to life; wars broke out forcing people to flee their homes.

Such problems aren't limited to the east. While most western European governments are the very model of social progressivism, welfare benefits have been slashed in recent years. And western Europe's booming economies have driven housing and land prices to record levels, effectively discouraging construction of low-income housing. As a result, poverty in western Europe is less glaring than that found elsewhere, but it is just as real.

While Habitat is not yet as active in Europe as it is in other parts of the world, its impact has nevertheless been profound. Habitat Northern Ireland has brought together Catholic and Protestant families to work side-by-side on construction. But old habits die hard. In Romania, after years of living under a repressive regime, people were skeptical of Habitat's motives; for that reason, there were only 34 applicants for the first eight houses built in Beius, despite the crushing need. The owner of the first house reported that people thought he must have bribed Habitat to get his house. Obviously, his only contribution was a small down payment and a lot of sweat. But gradually local people became convinced, and Romania is now home to one of the most active Habitat programs on the continent.

Still, unique obstacles remain. In Britain Habitat must compete with a host of other charities for donors' time and money. And the former communist countries don't have a broad-based tradition of volunteerism or philanthropy. But if Habitat can get Protestants and Catholics to work together in Belfast, there's no telling what it can do anyplace else in Europe—or the world.

Room for Improvement

These children live with their parents and aunt in a 440-square-foot apartment in Gliwice, **Poland**. Much of Habitat's work here and in other eastern European countries focuses on building houses with the many families who live in run-down, Soviet-era housing blocks. Such crowding often leads to health problems, domestic abuse, and poor school performance.

Half of the 3.8 million housing units in **Hungary** have severe infrastructure problems. This little girl lives with her mother in a run-down apartment in Budapest; the toilet, which they share with several neighbors, is down the hall. As substandard as such housing is, many Hungarians pay a huge percentage of their income for a tiny apartment.

"The Troubles" have plagued **Northern Ireland** with years of sectarian strife. Frequent bombings of homes—like this one in Belfast—have left much of the housing unusable and have further divided the country's Catholic and Protestant communities. Habitat has built more than 20 houses with families of both faiths.

Poland

Hungary

Northern Ireland

With Freedom, Uncertainty

The regime of Nicolae Ceausescu in Romania encouraged large families. (Two families, each with five children, live in the house shown at left.) As a result, after its fall, thousands of children were abandoned by families unable to cope. Overcrowded and decrepit orphanages turn these children onto the streets when they are 17 or 18 years old, without support or skills.

Habitat works with Romanian orphans, teaching them skills so they can support themselves.

Helping the Roma (gypsies), who are among Europe's most disenfranchised ethnic groups, is one of Habitat's goals. Roma families often live in squalor on the outskirts of towns and cities and are rarely granted the residency certification needed for housing, education, and health care.

Beius, Romania
Out of the Darkness

Ovidiu and Nicoleta Mara were just beginning their life together in 1989. The newlyweds squeezed into Ovi's tiny, 160-square-foot apartment in a factory-owned apartment building in the village of Beius. It was a tight fit, but the communist government had promised a larger apartment.

Then came December, and with it the fall of Nicolae Ceausescu's regime. Everything changed as the shock waves of post-communist life hit the country. Government money for new housing programs disappeared. Newly established private construction companies sprang up, but they weren't building low-income housing. Interest rates soared and mortgages did not exist. Rampant inflation and unemployment plagued the nation. At any other time, in any other place, the Maras, both university-educated engineers, would be considered middle class. But like so many Romanians, they found themselves locked into poverty housing—and locked out of economic stability.

Their hope for a better apartment disappeared. They would have to make do with the one room for the next several years, learning to get by with just its small sink and tiny stove. They shared a shower with the 17 other families on their floor, and they shared a toilet with 2 other families. Finally, as the economy worsened, the factory turned off the building's heat and hot water, making life even more unbearable for the residents in a country whose bitter winters can easily rival those of Minnesota.

But spring eventually arrived for the Maras, who today live in a Habitat house they built with their own hands,

part of a community of more than 20 Habitat homes in Beius. Ovi and Nico were among the first seven owners after working thousands of hours of sweat equity alongside their neighbors-to-be. "In two years of working together, we erased all kinds of differences—social, cultural, religious," says Nico. "What exists between us now is that we accept and understand each other.""

With the Carpathian Mountains in the distance, summer's vivid skies set off the bright red clay tile rooftops and white stucco exteriors of this new neighborhood on Habitat Street. Privacy, security, room to grow, and a spirit of community portend a brighter future not only for the Maras but for their town and country, too.

In 1996, Ovi and Nico Mara traveled with a group of Romanians to Vác, Hungary, as part of the Jimmy Carter Work Project. Habitat Romania was just a fledgling concept, and the Maras never dreamed that three years later they would become Habitat homeowners.

Hidden Poverty

Like most of western Europe, Portugal has enjoyed a great deal of economic growth since 1991, but the gap between rich and poor remains. Minimum-wage earners, particularly in the north, are likely to spend more than one-third of their income on shelters that lack basic utilities. There are an estimated 600,000 people living in substandard houses in Portugal.

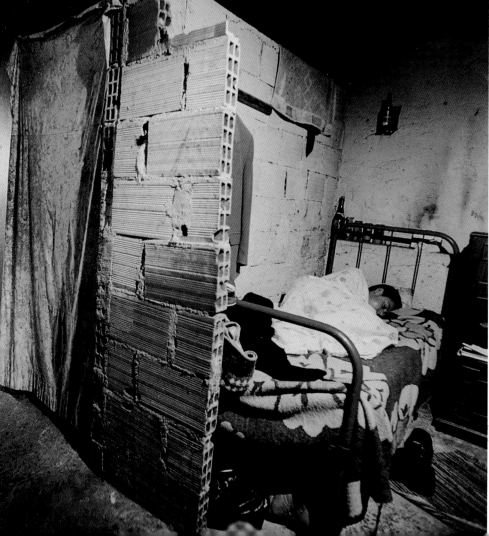

Habitat's work in Braga is based on promoting volunteerism, encouraging people to work together, and creating a sense of community.

In the northern city of Braga, as in much of Portugal, substandard housing is often hidden behind a seemingly decent exterior. Inside, there may be no running water, heat, sewerage, or electricity.

Braga, Portugal
The Rewards of Waiting

When Rosa Coelho gets up in the morning, the first thing she sees from her bedroom window is a shack she knows only too well. It is a place that is bitter cold in the winter, soaking wet in the rainy season, and dark and dank all year round. For more than two decades, she and her family called it home.

In 1977, Rosa and her husband, Fernando, were living in that shack when they began to build a house nearby for their young family. At first, Rosa's father-in-law helped with the construction, but after he died and Rosa's husband fell ill, the new house sat unfinished for years.

Mornings were bitter for Rosa as she raised her children, nursed her husband, and prayed for help. During the rainy season, when up to 80 inches of rain fall on this region, the interior of the shack was almost as wet as its exterior. Rosa swept the rainwater and mud from her frigid concrete floors in an exhausting, never-ending battle. She trudged uphill to pump water from a well and bathed her children in a bucket with water she heated over a fire; the family's only bathroom was a latrine several yards away. Rosa tended her garden and raised roosters, chickens, and pigs, which were housed in a small hut not much worse than her own.

Like so much of the country's inadequate housing, Rosa's shack—concealed behind a low hill next to her hog pen—isn't even visible from the main cobblestone street that runs through her tiny village of Cunha, just 45 minutes north of Braga, Portugal's third largest city. Just a stone's throw away from Rosa's property, upscale middle-class houses stand in harsh contrast to her old hut.

Because Rosa's government pension is only about US$170 a month, the likelihood was slim that she could afford new housing. But when she heard that Habitat for Humanity would begin work in Braga, she felt a small glimmer of hope. She applied to be the affiliate's second homeowner. Word came that Habitat would complete her house. Four months later, Rosa's husband died. Then one bright day, two groups of volunteers came from around the world to help finish the house. Rosa and her children, Miguel, 21, and Beatriz, 23, worked side-by-side with them.

Today, the shack the family once called home sits in the shadow of Rosa's new three-bedroom house, which has electricity, an indoor bathroom, a large kitchen, and hot and cold running water. Rosa greets mornings with a new perspective now. Explaining that she could never *(nunca!)* leave this house, she says: "I cannot say I had a house before, because I had only a shack. This is my first house. From here, my next home? The cemetery."

After years of living in a shack, Rosa Coelho now stands proudly in front of her new Habitat house with her son, Miguel.

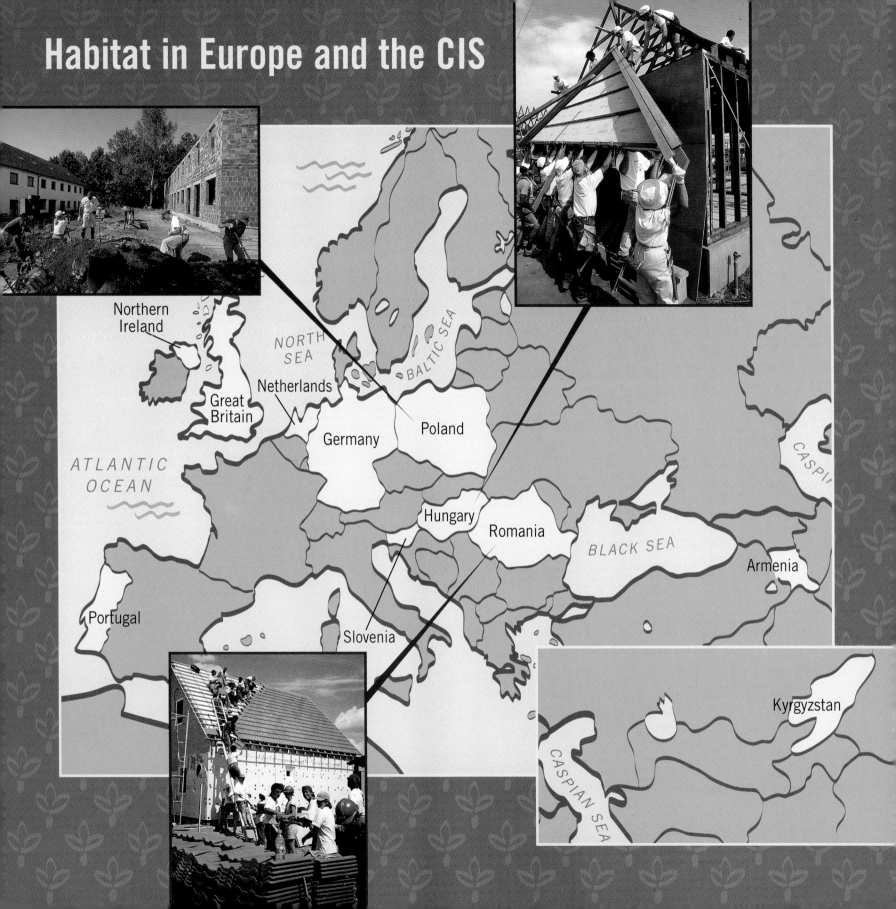

Habitat in Europe and the CIS

Northern Ireland

NORTH SEA

BALTIC SEA

Great Britain

Netherlands

Germany

Poland

ATLANTIC OCEAN

Hungary

Romania

BLACK SEA

CASPI

Armenia

Portugal

Slovenia

Kyrgyzstan

CASPIAN SEA

Armenia

Armenia, the smallest of the former Soviet republics, gained independence in 1991 and immediately undertook social and economic reforms. As those efforts unfolded, both income and unemployment levels remained critical issues through the 1990s, and satisfactory housing was well beyond the means even of many working families. A 1998 survey found that 50 percent of Armenians were living below the poverty line, many heavily dependent on assistance from relatives abroad to meet basic needs. It was in this climate that Habitat Armenia began working in early 2000, breaking ground for its first houses in Yerevan, the capital city.

HABITAT FACT: To minimize costs, Habitat Armenia is building with a readily available, indigenous stone.

Germany

Formally affiliated with HFHI since 1997, Habitat Germany brings together individuals and groups that support the organization's work. By offering material, financial, and volunteer support, HFH Germany aids programs in underdeveloped or developing countries where economic conditions make it particularly difficult for local communities to support a Habitat program.

HABITAT FACT: Volunteers with HFH Germany have helped convert old

buildings in the former East Berlin into clinics, as well as clothing and food centers for the homeless.

Great Britain

Thanks to an established, diversified economy and government assistance programs—including housing subsidies for many—the quality of life in Great Britain generally is quite high. Still, low-income families, particularly a growing population of immigrants, face challenges in finding and affording decent housing in a country where land for new housing is scarce and expensive. HFH Great Britain began in 1995 and is working through two affiliates, in the small town of Banbury and in the London borough of Southwark, to address those challenges. Six houses have been built in the first six years of work.

HABITAT FACT: Corporate partnerships have been instrumental in HFH Great Britain's work. Among the partners: United Airlines, The Body Shop International, the Redland Group, Persimmon Homes, Owens Corning, and Stanley Tools.

Hungary

HFH Hungary hosted the Jimmy Carter Work Project in 1996. The building of ten houses during that one-week event provided the impetus that has propelled HFH Hungary to become the biggest Habitat house-builder in Europe. Thirty-six houses were constructed between 1996 and 2000 as Hungary worked to make the transition from a planned to a market-driven economy. While lacking a tradition of volunteerism and private philanthropy to build upon, HFH Hungary is striving to forge strong relationships with government, church, business, and social sectors.

HABITAT FACT: HFH Hungary has two affiliates; HFHI'S Europe/CIS area office is in Budapest.

Kyrgyzstan

Kyrgyzstan is a country of breathtaking natural beauty and harsh economic decline. It has some of the highest mountains, largest lakes, and most remote wilderness areas in the world. It also has one of the highest infant mortality rates and lowest per capita incomes anywhere. Slightly more than half the population lives in poverty, earning less than US$20 a month. Substandard housing is prevalent throughout Kyrgyzstan, in both rural and urban areas, extending from the lowest socioeconomic levels well into the middle class. The

Habitat Kyrgyzstan Foundation was founded in February 1999 and was given a large parcel of land by the local city government, which was renamed "Habitat region." This land, a former apple orchard, contains plots for 50 houses, plus a small park. The first nine houses were scheduled for completion in the spring of 2001, with work to begin immediately on ten more.

HABITAT FACT: HFH Kyrgyzstan was the first Habitat affiliate in the former Soviet Union to begin construction of decent, affordable housing, and it is currently the only organization working on substandard housing issues in the country.

Netherlands

HFH Netherlands was founded in 1993 with the primary purposes of raising funds for overseas Habitat projects and recruiting volunteers for building teams

worldwide. A partnership has been formed with the Philippines. In addition to ongoing financial

Portugal

support from HFH Netherlands and Dutch businesses, more than 300 people from the Netherlands plan to participate in a 75-house build in the Philippines in summer 2001.

HABITAT FACT: While Habitat has not built any houses in the Netherlands, future building may be considered on islands of the Dutch Antilles.

Northern Ireland

In 1994, HFH Belfast/HFH Northern Ireland became the first Habitat affiliate in the United Kingdom. Exemplifying the fact that Habitat builds more than houses, HFH Belfast began with a vision of rebuilding houses, communities, and hope in an area that had witnessed years of violence between Catholics and Protestants. By 1997, 11 houses had been built in Iris Close, a predominantly Catholic West Belfast neighborhood, and by 2000, another 16 houses were completed in Glencairn Estate, a Protestant neighborhood just across a "peace line" and near Iris Close. In both neighborhoods, Catholic and Protestant volunteers worked side-by-side.

HABITAT FACT: Construction in Northern Ireland typically is done in multifamily rowhouse style, with brick walls and tile roofs.

Poland

Boasting one of the most successful transition economies in Europe after claiming independence from the Soviet Union in 1989, Poland nonetheless continues to have a low per-capita income, particularly given the high educational and skill levels of its citizens. Buying power is low, and general construction of new housing units has slowed considerably throughout the country. That slowdown has made decent housing increasingly difficult even for a family with an average monthly income to afford; for low-income residents, hope for improved housing is remote. HFH Poland's first affiliate was approved in 1992; by mid-2000, 16 Habitat houses had been built, new affiliates were forming, and plans were in place for a much accelerated building schedule. HFH Poland hopes to begin building 40 to 60 houses per year.

HABITAT FACT: International service teams from throughout Europe and the United States have been instrumental in helping HFH Poland build its initial houses.

Portugal

Though Portugal has a rich, diverse heritage, its economic growth has lagged behind that of other western European countries, and hidden poverty abounds in parts of the lushly scenic country. HFH Portugal began organizing in Braga in 1996 and built two houses in its first few years; at the same time it sought to build awareness of the Habitat program, the capacity to raise funds, and a general interest in the concept of volunteerism. Through a special Portugal Build 2000 initiative, 12 houses were built over a several-month period.

HABITAT FACT: HFH Portugal constructs houses modeled on traditional architecture and building styles, incorporating concrete column and beam construction in addition to light-gauge, metal-stud framing and drywall. A stucco exterior with red tile roofs completes the traditional look.

Romania

By some estimates, the housing need in Romania is approaching

Romania

a staggering one million units. In 1999, the United Nations Development Programme estimated that more than one-third of Romania's 22 million population lives under the threshold of poverty. Housing needs here are diverse, ranging from extremely overcrowded conditions in urban areas where multiple generations share tiny flats, to rural areas where thousands live in shacks that rival Third World conditions. Since 1996, Habitat Romania has worked to transform lives through decent shelter.

HABITAT FACT: In August 1999, hundreds of volunteers from the United States and Europe gathered to build ten houses in two weeks in Beius. The Eclipse Build coincided with the last solar eclipse of the millennium.

Slovenia

Once a part of communist Yugoslavia, Slovenia gained independence in 1991. The ensuing privatization process has not been a painless one. Market conditions have driven the price of housing well past the point of affordability for many ordinary citizens. The availability of new government housing is minimal, and many people are forced to live with their extended families, which can lead to extreme overcrowding.

HABITAT FACT: The first Habitat for Humanity affiliate in Slovenia was formed in 1997 in Ljubljana.

Latin America and the Caribbean

"More than houses, it has been my observation that [Habitat's] methodology builds self-esteem in families who otherwise would have the option only of living in cardboard houses.... It is a self-sustaining program which respects local culture and organization."

Estuardo Zapeta, anthropologist and journalist, Guatemala

Guatemala

Bolivia

Guyana

LATIN AMERICA AND THE CARIBBEAN

Creating Hope

So much of what Habitat for Humanity International deals with is new. New homes, new beginnings, new hope. But in Latin America and the Caribbean, the biggest challenge Habitat faces dates back to the founding of the nations themselves: Who controls the land?

Land ownership colors housing issues throughout most of Central and South America and much of the Caribbean. The majority of arable land is controlled by a very small percentage of the population, while the rural poor own virtually none. Sixty percent of the arable land in Brazil, for example, is owned by less than 2 percent of the population, while 70 percent of rural families own no land at all. Title issues compound the problem. As a result of unstable governments and sporadic waves of land reform, several people may have legitimate claims to the same piece of land.

And so the dispossessed of the region flock to the cities, which are growing at an astonishing rate. More than half of all the residents of the Dominican Republic now live in cities, twice as many as in 1960, while 70 percent of Colombians are now urban dwellers. As cities grow, land in and around metropolitan areas becomes more expensive, often rising beyond the reach of even middle-class residents.

The result is a dire shortage of acceptable housing, so more and more people crowd into squatter settlements, or *pueblos jovenes* (young towns), as they are known in Peru. The sprawling shanty-towns of São Paulo alone house more people than does Brazil's capital, Brasilia. Officials estimate that one in three families either lack housing or live in substandard housing and 43 percent of the population lack access to adequate sanitation.

Guatemala

Bolivia

LATIN AMERICA AND THE CARIBBEAN

Habitat has been active in the region since building its first house there, in Guatemala, in 1979. Its affiliates in 22 countries have built some 35,000 homes, with more than 11,000 in Mexico. Initially, much of the work was done in rural areas, where Habitat houses with sturdy roofs and masonry construction went a long way to prevent Chagas disease, an ailment spread by an insect that lives in thatch roofs and mud walls. But as populations in the region continue to migrate to urban areas, Habitat has become more active there, partnering with other service organizations such as World Vision and expanding into development areas that reach beyond housebuilding—infrastructure and micro-credit in particular.

Disaster response has become an important part of Habitat's mission in the region. The shantytowns that are clustered around every major city are especially vulnerable to the earthquakes, floods, and volcanic eruptions that plague many areas, especially in Central America. Habitat built 387 houses in Honduras with families displaced by Hurricane Mitch in 1998. And work is proceeding on 727 houses for Salvadorans affected by the devastating earthquakes of January and February 2001.

Habitat also constructs affordable housing in island resort areas such as Tobago, Jamaica, the Dominican Republic, and Antigua, where the high cost of importing materials and stringent building codes present a challenge.

The region's problems aren't insurmountable. Pablo Neruda, the poetic conscience of South America, wrote in his memoirs, "I continue to work with the materials I have, the materials I am made of." The same can be said of Habitat's efforts throughout Latin America and the Caribbean. Habitat recognizes that it is within its people, its land, and its spirit that the solutions lie.

Abiding Poverty

Habitat has built more homes in **Mexico** than in any country other than the United States. That's because the need for housing in Mexico is so dramatic. Private homes are expensive, and it's still hard for the average Mexican to secure a mortgage. Habitat's 17 affiliates in Mexico build in cities, rural areas, and everywhere in between, using local materials that help hold down the cost of construction.

Almost one-fourth of **Chile's** population lives below the poverty line, and there are almost one thousand low-income neighborhoods or squatter areas in the country. Rapidly rising prices and the high cost of living make it difficult, if not impossible, for many families to satisfy even their most basic needs.

Habitat faces some distinctive challenges working in Caribbean countries with tourism-based economies, such as **Antigua**, Jamaica, and Tobago. Land tends to be very expensive, as are construction supplies, many of which must be imported. And codes intended to make homes more hurricane-resistant can put building costs out of the reach of the poor.

84 ONE FAMILY AT A TIME

Mexico

Chile

Antigua

A Makeshift Existence

Brazil is the largest country in South America, larger even than the continental United States. Its housing problems are outsized, too. A 1995 study found that nearly five million Brazilian homes were substandard; some 100,000 Brazilians are without any kind of shelter, many living under bridges and in culverts. Most cities have extensive and notoriously crowded *favelas*—shantytowns of huts made from pieces of wood, plastic sheeting, and packing materials. Such intense overcrowding is only likely to increase as urban land becomes ever more expensive and Brazil's young population (28 percent of Brazilians are under 15 years of age) continues to swell.

Habitat Piracicaba does more than build houses. Its education programs provide information on cooperative action, homeownership, and problem-solving skills.

Piracicaba, Brazil
Little by Little

Like millions of working people living in Brazil's cities, Maria and Jonas Roberto barely got through the country's 1994 economic crisis, during which the annual rate of inflation passed 2,000 percent. At the height of the recession, fully one in three Brazilians was living in poverty. Forced to choose between feeding their families and paying rent, the least fortunate migrated to the makeshift shacks in the crime-ridden *favelas* that ring Brazil's modern cities.

The Robertos were able to avoid such a fate, thanks in part to Habitat. Maria, a maid, and Jonas, a car painter, lived with their five children in a rental house in a safe, decent neighborhood. They watched as their rent rose to 60 percent of their income, a hardship they were able to endure—until Maria lost her job. They fell behind in rent payments and went into debt to avoid moving the children away from their schools, friends, and extended family. "I wanted my children to get a good education," says Maria. "And I didn't want my daughter to have to clean floors like I do." Food grew scarcer; so did shoes and clothes. "We were desperate," recalls Jonas. "All we could do was work and pray." Then a relative read about the local Habitat program.

For the next 14 months, the Robertos spent their weekends and holidays building up 2,000 hours of sweat equity for their Habitat house. They proudly tell how their oldest boy, Elisio, then 11, cooked meals and looked after the younger children while his parents worked. "Pulling together around this house has made our whole family stronger," says Jonas. "Now we don't worry about paying such high rent. And we can give the children the love and attention they need."

Today the Robertos live in a three-bedroom Habitat house in Conjunto Mario Dedini, a neighborhood where Habitat has built 244 homes since 1995. They pay about one-tenth of their former rent on a 17-year mortgage. There's a good school up the road, and a soccer field, and several churches within walking distance. Maria has a full-time job at a local supermarket and the family can afford food and clothes and has even added onto the house. "In Portuguese, there is a saying, *'pouco a pouco,'* little by little," she says. "That's how we're building our new life. The money we pay every month now goes toward our own house, not someone else's."

The Robertos' new house has a tiny front yard. During the day, children play there, kick balls in the street, or fly kites in a nearby soccer field.

Lives Devastated

Just before noon on January 13, 2001, a powerful earthquake registering 7.6 on the Richter scale shook El Salvador, one of the Western Hemisphere's poorest countries and one still reeling from the effects of Hurricane Mitch in 1998. In the 40 seconds or so that the ground rippled and flipped, damage to the country was profound. No towns were untouched; some were utterly destroyed. Exactly one month later, on February 13, a second major earthquake, registering 6.2 on the Richter scale, struck the country. The combined damage of both earthquakes left 1,127 dead, 7,660 injured, and 310,000 homes damaged or destroyed. Habitat's six Salvadoran affiliates have vowed to help the nation rebuild, promising to construct in 14 months more than 700 homes made of concrete blocks and roofed with fiber cement sheeting or concrete tiles—homes that will better withstand natural disasters. The sign on the left commemorates victims of the quake. It reads, in part, "Here is my family's house.... They will live inside me for the rest of my life."

After the earthquakes, Salvadorans were joined by Habitat volunteers from Nicaragua, Canada, Costa Rica, Guatemala, Honduras, Northern Ireland, and the United States to rebuild their country.

San Vicente, El Salvador
Strong as Faith

Two weeks after the most lethal earthquake to hit El Salvador in 15 years jarred the lives of countless Salvadoran families, a small group of people met in the shade of a makeshift tarp in the village of San Vicente to alter the lives of six families. But this time the change would be, mercifully, for the better: The villagers had gathered for a ceremony to dedicate six new Habitat for Humanity houses and to turn over the keys to the families that would occupy them. The houses were almost complete when the earthquake struck, and even though almost 70 percent of the town's dwellings were rendered uninhabitable, the Habitat houses weren't even scratched.

"I feel very happy but at the same time sad for all of our brothers," says Natividad de Mercedez Hernandez, one of the new homeowners. "My neighbor's house exploded, and the entire roof fell in." She points to the severely damaged house next to hers, much of it reduced to a pile of rubble. The terror of the quake remains with her. "I felt as if the earth was going to swallow me," she recalls, explaining how the ground shook and the streets moved like an ocean. She prayed to the Lord to pardon her sins because she thought the end was near.

Eventually the shaking stopped. Although her previous house—a one-room adobe shelter shared by seven people—hadn't come crashing down around her, the walls had opened up and the roof beam was cracked. "We couldn't live there," she says. "It isn't habitable now." So she and her family moved into their nearly completed Habitat house just a few hours after the earthquake struck.

As her neighbor, Juan Carlos, worked to save some of the remaining adobe blocks from the ruins of his home, Natividad, her husband, and their four children stood outside of their solid home made of concrete blocks, built to better withstand earthquakes. Says Natividad, who still volunteers with Habitat to help other community members build their houses, "Habitat for me…is a miracle."

The Hernandez family was lucky: Both they
and their Habitat house survived two earthquakes
while homes all around them were destroyed.

Habitat in Latin America and the Caribbean

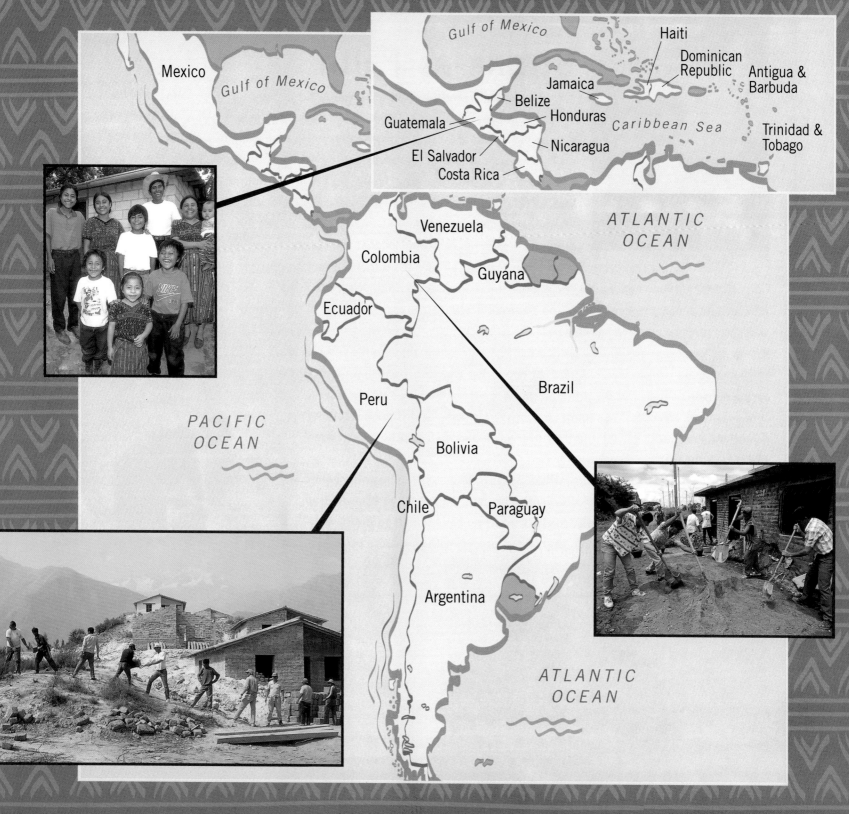

Gulf of Mexico

Mexico

Gulf of Mexico

Haiti

Dominican Republic

Jamaica

Belize

Guatemala

Honduras

Caribbean Sea

El Salvador

Nicaragua

Costa Rica

Antigua & Barbuda

Trinidad & Tobago

Venezuela

ATLANTIC OCEAN

Colombia

Guyana

Ecuador

Peru

Brazil

PACIFIC OCEAN

Bolivia

Chile

Paraguay

Argentina

ATLANTIC OCEAN

Antigua and Barbuda

Located in the heart of the Caribbean, Antigua and Barbuda is a small, twin nation. Its beautiful beaches attract thousands of tourists each year, but few see the inadequate living conditions in the interior, home to many of the nation's families. HFHI was invited to assist in providing homes here after the devastation wrought by Hurricanes Luis and Marilyn in 1995. An affiliate was approved in 1997.

HABITAT FACT: Jointly financing local projects with HFHI, which has covered much of its local start-up expenses, HFH Antigua/Barbuda has grown into a strong, sustainable national program.

Argentina

Argentina is South America's second-largest country. It has abundant natural resources and a literate population, but its economy has experienced volatility since the onset of a national-debt crisis in the late 1980s. HFHI's housing program was introduced in 1992, and six houses were built. Following a long period of

Brazil

inactivity, HFH Argentina was reactivated in late 2000.

HABITAT FACT: HFH Argentina is developing affiliates in the city of Lujan, two hours northeast of Buenos Aires, and in the northwest suburbs of the capital city.

Belize

HFH Belize was approved as a partnering country of HFHI in 1999, and the first house was completed in December of that year in Belize City. Belize is a scenic getaway for vacationers, yet it is also home to extreme poverty. Studies have found that for every 100 homes in rural Belize, 25 are without a safe and adequate water supply and 65 are without safe means of human waste disposal.

HABITAT FACT: Due to the city's subtropical climate and low-lying land, Habitat houses in Belize City are built of concrete block on a raised foundation.

Bolivia

HFH Bolivia began work in 1985, with help from the Methodist Church and in partnership with homesteaders in the Alto Beni region. By 2000, affiliates were operating in eight communities, and over 2,400 houses had been built. An estimated two-thirds of Bolivians live in poverty. Getting legal titles to lots on which to build, even for families that can afford a Habitat mortgage payment, is a routine problem here.

Antigua

HABITAT FACT: The sturdy roofs and masonry construction used here act as a buffer against an insect that thrives in the mud walls and thatch roofs of shacks, and spreads Chagas disease.

Brazil

Throughout this sprawling land, at least 20 million people live in substandard housing, about two-thirds of them in urban areas. HFH Brazil was founded in 1987 and now has active Habitat affiliates in both urban and rural areas. Some 1,300 houses had been built by the end of 2000.

HABITAT FACT: HFH Brazil received the "Premio Bem Eficiente de 1999," an award recognizing Brazilian nonprofit organizations that have demonstrated high standards of work, organization, and administration.

Chile

Despite improving economic conditions because of increased foreign trade, an estimated 22 percent of Chile's population lives below the poverty line. In 1999, the housing deficit was estimated at 800,000 houses. The overwhelming majority of residents have no access to land for building houses. HFH Chile was formed in late 2000, with initial efforts focused on securing land.

HABITAT FACT: Leaders of HFH Chile are committed to designing homes that are extremely economical to build, buy, and maintain.

Colombia

In the last two decades of the 20th century, Colombia's cities experienced explosive growth. A building boom ensued, and the cost of land, building materials, and skilled construction labor escalated. One of the major challenges in Colombia is containing building costs so that houses are affordable. Habitat Colombia began in 1994 and had built 313 houses by the end of 2000.

HABITAT FACT: As of 2001, HFH Colombia has five affiliates, including one in Quimbaya, where Habitat's work is primarily with low-income coffee farmers.

Costa Rica

HFHI began work in the Costa Rican town of Esparza in 1987 and completed 50 houses in its first three years. When the government began an ambitious housing program for the poor in

Bolivia

1991, Habitat stopped its work in the country. In 1996, however, following cutbacks in the government program, community leaders in the town of San Ramón invited Habitat to begin work again in Costa Rica. By 2001, 191 houses had been built.

HABITAT FACT: In 1998, Habitat's Latin America/Caribbean Area Office was moved from HFHI headquarters in Americus, Georgia, to San Jose, Costa Rica, as part of a decentralization initiative.

Dominican Republic

In the mid-1990s, the Dominican Republic's housing deficit was estimated at 600,000 homes. With the damage sustained from Hurricane Georges in 1998, that number rose dramatically. HFH Dominican Republic began working in 1987 in and around the southwestern city of Barahona, an area where many people live in shacks made of wood and sheets of rusty tin. For most of them, without a program such as Habitat, owning a secure home would remain only a dream.

HABITAT FACT: Habitat houses in the Dominican Republic are built to withstand hurricanes.

Ecuador

Ecuador's housing deficit is estimated at 1.2 million and has been increasing by at least 50,000 houses per year. Ecuador experienced profound economic crises after El Niño inflicted more than US$3 billion in damages in 1998; inflation rates soared and exports plunged. HFH Ecuador was recognized in early 1998 and by 2000 had built 28 houses.

HABITAT FACT: Habitat houses in Ecuador are constructed of hurricane- and flood-resistant materials.

El Salvador

El Salvador, the smallest and most densely populated of the Central American countries, has survived much and still faces huge challenges. Following a civil war that claimed more than 75,000 lives between 1980 and 1992, poverty and the need for housing became extreme. The devastation left in the wake of Hurricane Mitch in 1998 compounded the housing crisis.

Habitat began its work here in 1993 and undertook new initiatives following the hurricane; by the end of 2000 it had built 1,352 houses. In early 2001, Habitat immediately began working in communities affected by two massive earthquakes.

HABITAT FACT: HFH El Salvador is in the process of changing construction materials to make them more environmentally sustainable. Affiliates now use industrial tubing and cinder block, not wood and kiln-fired brick.

Guatemala

An estimated 80 percent of Guatemala's population lives in poverty, 50 percent of them in extreme poverty, and the housing deficit is about 1.5 million nationwide. The situation was intensified by the widespread devastation delivered by Hurricane Mitch in 1998. Through 2000, HFH Guatemala had built over 7,800 houses.

HABITAT FACT: Habitat houses in Guatemala are designed to be disaster resistant, with concrete floors, block walls, and corrugated-zinc roofs.

Guyana

With a per-capita income of less than one-fifth the South American average, Guyana is one of the world's poorest countries. Government statistics indicate that more than 20 percent of the Guyanese people are in need of housing. Established in 1995,

HFH Guyana dedicated its first six houses in 1997 and through 2000 had built 107 homes.

HABITAT FACT: HFH Guyana houses, built of hurricane-resistant concrete materials, have two bedrooms and plumbing but no electricity.

Haiti

Buffeted by political instability, an underdeveloped economy, and social unrest, Haiti may be the poorest country in the Western Hemisphere. With nearly 80 percent of Haitians living in poverty, housing needs are great. Habitat has been at work here since 1981 and by 2000 had built nearly 400 houses.

HABITAT FACT: Habitat houses in Haiti are built of clay brick with cement roofs or of cement block with corrugated-tin roofs.

Honduras

Just as Honduras was beginning to experience moderate economic growth, in 1998 Hurricane Mitch delivered a stunning blow: an estimated US$3 billion in total damage, 75,000 homes destroyed,

Guatemala

and 165,000 homes seriously damaged in a matter of hours. Habitat for Humanity, which had been building houses in Honduras since 1988, accelerated the pace of its work with the help of designated corporate and individual gifts, and by the end of 2000 it had built 2,291 homes.

HABITAT FACT: Habitat began work here in 1988 in the Yure River Valley, initiated through Proyecto Aldea Global, which focuses on development in agriculture, health, education, and community.

Jamaica

HFH Jamaica began work in 1993 with the goal of alleviating a housing crisis caused by high interest rates, skyrocketing land prices, and shrinking employment and real wages. Recent estimates show that about one-third of Jamaica's population continues to live below the poverty line. As a result, without a program such as Habitat, homeownership would be impossible for many.

HABITAT FACT: Most HFH Jamaica houses employ concrete-block construction reinforced with steel.

Mexico

The third-largest and most populous Spanish-speaking country in Latin America, Mexico is economically diverse. But the housing deficit is enormous: An estimated one-third of all adults in Mexico live in substandard conditions. Habitat has been working in Mexico since 1987

Jamaica

and by 2000 had built 11,050 houses, making it the largest HFH program outside the United States.

HABITAT FACT: Despite several natural disasters, including a 7.2 earthquake that shook Mexico City in 1999 and Hurricane Pauline in 1997, no HFH home in Mexico has been lost to natural disaster.

Nicaragua

Nicaragua, the largest country in Central America, has had a troubled recent history. A civil war in the 1980s pushed the country to the brink of financial ruin. Although the political situation stabilized in the 1990s, economic damages remained high. One study in the late 1990s indicated that nearly 75 percent of Nicaraguans were living in poverty, more than 55 percent were unemployed, and 69 percent were living in unsanitary conditions. HFH Nicaragua started in 1984 and through 2000 had built 1,767 houses.

HABITAT FACT: A 100-house project

in Matagalpa is aiding victims of Hurricane Mitch. It includes a school and a health center, in addition to house construction.

Paraguay

Recent studies estimate the housing deficit in Paraguay at more than 350,000 units. Overcrowding affects about 30 percent of the population. HFH Paraguay's first affiliate was formed in mid-1998 in Asunción. By the end of 2000, 36 houses had been built.

HABITAT FACT: Habitat houses in Paraguay are built of bricks and roof tiles made of local materials.

Peru

Despite improvements in Peru's economy through the 1990s, about half the population still lives below the poverty line, and the need for housing has been exacerbated by massive migrations from rural areas to urban centers. HFH Peru began work in 1982 and through 2000 had built 4,700 houses.

HABITAT FACT: Two Habitat communities have been built in Tacna. One includes more than 500 houses, as well as a church, a school, and a medical clinic.

Trinidad and Tobago

HFHI teamed in 1994 with a Trinidad organization called the Foundation for the Enhancement and Enrichment of Life to begin addressing local housing needs. HFH Trinidad and Tobago was

officially recognized in 1996 and through 2000 had built 25 Habitat houses.

HABITAT FACT: HFH Trinidad and Tobago dedicated its first home in 1997, with the prime minister and his wife on hand for the ceremony.

Venezuela

Despite the country's healthy oil industry and growing political stability, modest wage increases make it difficult for most Venezuelans to cope with inflation rates that have reached as high as 30 percent annually. Nearly 50 percent of the population lives below the poverty line. Devastating floods and mud

Peru

slides struck Venezuela in December 1999, leaving thousands homeless. HFH Venezuela was formed in November 2000 through the initiative of local leaders and with support from HFHI's Disaster Response Office.

HABITAT FACT: HFH Venezuela houses are designed with two bedrooms, a bathroom, a kitchen, and a living area.

United States
and Canada

"The genius of Habitat is that it not only transforms the lives of the new homeowners but it changes the lives of those who do the work as well."

Robert Adams, former Executive Director

National Low Income Housing Coalition

California

Tennessee

R.M. BROOKS
GEN. MDSE.
GROCERIES   DRY GOODS   NOTIONS

TOURIST INFO.

ICE

PEPSI

Coca-Cola

Colorado

UNITED STATES AND CANADA

Fulfilling the Dream

It's a nice idea that everyone in the United States and Canada lives in a comfortable house and has plenty to eat, but it's certainly not true. While homeownership in the United States is at an all-time high, with two-thirds of families living in a dwelling they can call their own, the means of homeownership—and sometimes of just basic shelter—have never been farther out of reach for the remaining one third. The North American economy boomed in the late 1990s, but in recent decades the United States has had a de facto two-tier wage system in which educated workers' earnings increased while the wages of the unskilled stagnated. Since 1975, almost all the gains in income have gone to the wealthiest 20 percent of households. The result is that of the United States' 281 million residents, 32 million live below the poverty line, and 5.4 million cannot find a decent place to live at a price they can afford.

These disparities are especially evident in housing. The average cost of a new home in America is at an all-time high ($205,000 in 2000, up from $176,000 in just three years), and desirable land for building is at a premium. Rents have soared as the stock of affordable housing has plummeted—by 1.3 million units from 1996 to 1998 alone as the federal government cut funding for public housing. The one million low-income families seeking public housing face an average wait of almost one year; in New York City it is eight years, and in Oakland, California, six. And the problem isn't limited to the cities. One-third of the families in the most dire need of housing live in suburbs, while the highest proportion of substandard housing is in rural areas. The situation is worse for some ethnic groups. Forty percent of housing is substandard on reservations, home for half of all Native Americans.

Florida

North Carolina

For many low-income families, Habitat for Humanity offers the only practical alternative to being trapped in substandard or high-rent housing. Since building its first house in the United States, in San Antonio, Texas, in 1978, Habitat has done much to address these problems. Like ripples spreading across a pond, it has grown to encompass more than 1,600 affiliates working in all 50 states and its territories and all 10 Canadian provinces. It is now the fifteenth-largest house-builder in the United States, where a typical Habitat house costs its owner just less than $50,000. Through 2000, it had built and rehabilitated more than 35,000 homes—with Native Hawaiians on homestead land, with migrant workers in Florida, with the urban poor in New York, with the rural poor in the Mississippi Delta. Habitat understands the importance of providing housing for families with young children, because children are more likely to live in poverty than any other age group. The United States' child poverty rate is often two to three times higher than that of most Western industrialized nations. Habitat helps children avoid many of the problems associated with growing up in substandard dwellings: a host of health issues including emotional and psychological problems, and poor school performance.

Most of Habitat's work has been in rural and suburban areas, where land to build on is more readily available, but there is an increasing emphasis on urban environments. City projects often involve renovation of abandoned dwellings rather than new construction, which makes it more likely that communities will remain intact. Regardless of the location of its projects, Habitat in the United States and Canada has made the dream of owning a home closer to reality for thousands of people, brick by brick.

Through the Cracks

More Americans than ever before live in metropolitan areas. This has driven up the cost of housing, particularly for low-income families. Habitat for Humanity works with community groups in Baltimore, **Maryland**, to restore the city's rowhouses and provide homes for low-income workers.

Ninety children are born into poverty in the United States every hour. Habitat's 63 affiliates in **Kentucky** have built almost 900 houses that shelter hundreds of children.

Almost 10 percent of housing units are either moderately or severely inadequate, like the one this family inhabited in **Georgia** before the Jimmy Carter Work Project helped them construct a new dwelling. Some 21 percent of rural residents pay enough for housing to be considered cost-burdened; this expense is especially hard on renters.

The sky-high price of land in **Hawaii** means that affordable housing is often beyond the reach of the working poor. In extreme situations, some families are forced to live entirely outdoors, with tarpaulins serving as their roofs.

Urban Decay

In the 1930s and 1940s, Baltimore's African-American neighborhood of Sandtown was full of shops, thriving businesses, and theaters like the Royal, where Billie Holiday and other jazz greats sang. But after riots in the 1960s ignited many American cities, most of Sandtown's businesses and middle-class families fled to the suburbs. When they left, shops closed, schools were boarded up, and houses were sold to absentee landlords. Those who remained tended to be poor; they soon found their paychecks replaced by unemployment checks. By the late 1980s, Sandtown was filled with dilapidated houses, many of them vacant and prey to vandals.

Habitat has restored more than 160 units in Sandtown, and another 50 are under rehabilitation.

Sandtown residents faced tough choices. They could continue renting the old houses, where unsafe stairways, faulty heating and plumbing, toxic lead-based paint, overcrowding, and evictions were a part of daily life. Or they could abandon their community, as others had. Many chose to stay. When a Habitat affiliate was formed in 1989, it focused on a 12-block part of the 72-square-block neighborhood, buying and restoring old houses and building new ones.

Baltimore, Maryland
Coming Home

When Antoine Bennett left Sandtown in 1989 to serve a prison sentence, the 18-year-old thought of himself as a steely young man. He didn't have much choice. His mother had died when he was seven months old, and his father had stepped into his life only occasionally. His grandmother had raised him and his twin brother in one of Sandtown's old rowhouses, where as many as ten family members were forced to share just two bedrooms.

During his four years in prison, Antoine dreamed of a more decent life. "Being in prison showed me what death was like," he says. "It takes you away from human touch, human concern, and human compassion. I promised myself I would leave that place smarter than when I came in, get my GED, and make something of my life."

Antoine is back in Sandtown—in a home of his own. After working for two years to build up 430 hours of sweat equity, Antoine became a Habitat homeowner in 1996. He lives in a renovated Habitat rowhouse and works as a job counselor. He pays a modest amount for the mortgage on his comfortable three-bedroom, two-bath home, which he shares with a brother and a cousin. Surrounded by the friends and family he grew up with, Antoine says that he realizes how lucky he was to have a community to come home to.

Antoine also says that he loves his Habitat house—including the small deck, the grassy backyard, and the basement he has set up as a den. But his biggest blessing, he notes, is the nurturing environment it provides for his extended family of brothers, cousins, and nieces. Now, Sunday dinners with friends, sleep-overs for the children, and backyard barbecues with relatives are regular happenings at Antoine's. Instinctively, he is creating a safehouse for the next generation, something he wishes more men in Sandtown would do. "I want to keep the children tight and growing up together, surrounded by people who know them and love them," he says. "Maybe if I had had that kind of experience when I was growing up, I would have put family before the streets. There are a lot of women on the front lines holding families together these days. We men need to be there, too. And thanks to organizations like Habitat, we can."

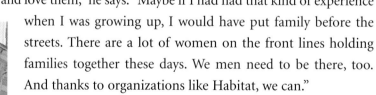

Habitat's cost-effective construction and renovation techniques, as well as the hard work of many volunteers and homeowners, spared Sandtown's elegant rowhouses from the wrecking ball.

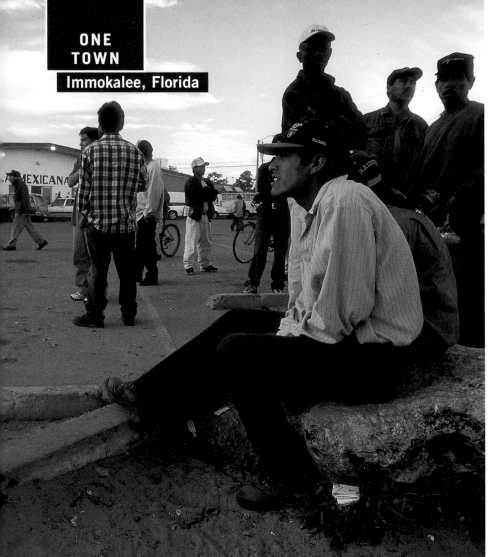

Wanted: A Future

Every October, the population of Immokalee, a farming town in southwest Florida, swells from 8,000 people to more than 20,000 as migrant farm workers come to harvest the winter tomato crop. Immokalee is the state's largest—and poorest—farm worker community. Most of the laborers are from Mexico, Central America, and the Caribbean; on a good day, they can earn as much as ten times here what they could at home. But there's no guarantee that they will find work, or shelter, in a town where the demand for both can quickly exceed supply. Even the most decrepit trailers can command $400 to $800 per month in season.

The Habitat affiliate formed in Immokalee in 1978 had built 202 houses by 2000.

A Father's Dream Comes True

Juan and Lupe Garcia grew up as migrant workers, his family from Texas, hers from Mexico. They know well the hardscrabble life of following the seasonal harvest of crops in the United States, constantly moving from place to place. They remember summers on the road, sleeping in the car, toting heavy loads, watching their parents hustle to make ends meet. When Juan met Lupe picking oranges in Immokalee, he vowed to get her out of the fields and to keep their children from such a transient existence. He won a college scholarship and attended classes during the day, working nights and weekends to pay the rent. But when Lupe got laid off from her job in the fields because of a freeze, money grew tight and Juan saw his dreams fading fast.

In 1978, Juan heard Millard Fuller speak to a group of Immokalee farm workers about Habitat. "Ironically, the town's name comes from the Seminole word meaning 'my home,'" says Fuller. "That's the one thing that's completely out of the reach of most migrant workers." Juan knew that the stability of growing up in a home their parents owned would help farm workers' children get the most important thing they needed to build a better future: an education. Even when their parents went north to harvest crops, the children could stay in one place and go to school. So Juan served on the first board of Immokalee Habitat and in 1980, after contributing 2,000 hours of sweat equity, he moved Lupe and their young son, Noel, into a Habitat house.

The fields are long behind the Garcias today. Juan works at a tropical fish farm and Lupe owns a manicure business; they'll soon pay off the mortgage on their house. Juan likes to show guests Noel's trophy-filled bedroom, immensely proud of the fact that his son was the valedictorian of Immokalee High School's class of 1995 and went on to become the family's first graduate of a four-year college. Noel is equally proud of his dad. "My father instilled in me the fact that without an education, you will never turn your dreams into reality," he says. Now Noel's younger sister, Sylvia, is looking forward to college as well.

The Habitat affiliate founded in Immokalee is now the most active builder of single-family homes in the community, thanks in part to volunteers from nearby Naples, one of the wealthiest retirement communities in the United States.

The Face of Rural Poverty

Much of Habitat's work in the United States takes place in rural areas because a variety of factors intertwine to cause housing problems there. Agricultural or forestry jobs tend to be seasonal and low-paying. And the beauty of many of these communities draws tourists who drive up land and housing prices while at the same time creating low-paying service jobs that are seasonal at best. The result: Almost 10 percent of America's rural housing is either moderately or severely inadequate. Michigan's Newyago County, one of the state's poorest, is one such area. Habitat has worked there since 1992.

In some of Michigan's rural areas, Habitat for Humanity is building the first new houses in 50 years.

A House Is Good Medicine

When Karen and Ted Taylor moved to White Cloud in 1990, they began to build the life they always wanted. They rented a rambling, old house big enough to hold them and their children. They found decent jobs, and the kids were happy. Things looked pretty good. But their lives took a harsh turn when Karen was diagnosed with leukemia and her doctors told her that she had just 18 months to live.

Ted scrambled to keep the family together. He held down his job as a cook while caring for the children and Karen, and he drove her 250 miles every week to Detroit for overnight hospital treatments. But without Karen's income, the Taylors had trouble meeting their rent and were denied a mortgage when they tried to buy their house.

The Taylors managed to scrape together $500 to buy a decrepit mobile home on a half-acre lot. But the electricity in their new home was faulty, the kitchen leaked, and the accumulated mold overwhelmed Karen's weakened immune system. She was hospitalized twice that winter with pneumonia.

Then an acquaintance told Habitat about the Taylors' plight. He urged Karen and Ted to apply for a home; they were accepted and contributed 500 hours of sweat equity. A local bank donated a vacant house a few miles away and arranged for it to be trucked to the Taylors' land, where Habitat workers renovated it. The family moved into the cozy, three-bedroom brick house in 1993.

Things are looking up for the family in other ways, too. In 1998, Ted opened his own restaurant, Taylor's Chalet, in nearby Brohman. With the help of his two youngest children, he's been able to expand into catering. Karen's health remains fragile, but she still volunteers on Habitat's family selection committee. "I always remind new families that this county is poor, but very giving," she says. "Thanks to Habitat, we have a warm, safe, comfortable home with low mortgage payments. We've been able to build the dream we wanted, the dream Ted wanted, and the dream the kids want for their lives. That's what means the most to us."

With the stability of a decent home, the Taylors could turn their energy and attention to work and education, and improved medical care for Karen.

Home at Last

Rudys Rivas will never forget the last months before she fled her homeland. In 1984, El Salvador was in the midst of a bitter civil war. Soldiers searching for guerrillas killed her daughter, sister, and step-father. Her mother disappeared a year later. In fear of her own life, Rudys bundled up her son and took him to her sister in a neighboring village. She promised to send for the boy, then began a frightening, 2,000-mile journey to Kitchener, Ontario, to join her brother and

other Salvadoran refugees. Rudys found asylum there, but it was just the start of her odyssey: She was homeless, spoke only Spanish, and had given birth to a daughter on her journey.

Friends helped her find a small apartment in a government housing project and arrange for her son to immigrate. Rudys was grateful, yet she longed for what she had lost. "I told myself that someday, I'm going to have a little house with a big backyard where it's quiet, and there are no sounds of gunshots, and I can plant fruit trees and grow vegetables," she recalls. She worked as a maid and studied English. Eventually she landed a job in a factory. Yet every time her income went up, so did her rent. One night, after years of living in government housing, she heard about Habitat on a television show. She was certain that she, a single mother, would never be chosen, yet she applied anyway. She was accepted.

In the summer of 2000, an incredulous Rudys and her two teenagers found themselves in the middle of Habitat's first Canadian Women Build. The Waterloo affiliate had combed Ontario for female excavators, concrete workers, framers, electricians, plumbers, roofers, and landscapers to join in a two-week blitz build. All told, 200 volunteers, ages 20 to 60, participated, including Habitat's cofounder Linda Fuller, mother of the Women Build program.

Rudys's daughter, Linda, comments that the women probably will never know how much their contribution— and the secure, one-story, 1,040-square-foot bungalow the family now calls home—means to her mother. "She loves this house," she says. "I often catch her just sitting on the sofa, smiling and saying to herself, 'I'm home. I'm finally home.'" After seeing humanity at its worst, Rudys feels that she now has seen it at its best. "These women give love, and they don't ask me for anything in return," she says. "It comes from the heart. I can tell."

Rudys Rivas and her family have a place to call their own, thanks to the work of the female volunteers who were part of the first Canadian Women Build.

Refuge Required

It seems fitting that Canada's first Women Build gave a woman who had to flee her homeland and had struggled alone as a single mother for 14 years a refuge at last. As in many developed nations, Habitat Canada faces the difficult challenge of overcoming outmoded ideas about the nature of poverty. Habitat workers in many First World countries find that potential donors and volunteers are often surprised to learn that their country is home to poor people who might need help getting a good roof over their heads. In industrialized nations, poverty often has a low profile, and the need may not be as abject and readily apparent as it is in parts of Asia and Latin America. Yet it is still acute as more people become part of the "working poor."

ONE TOWN

Kitchener, Ontario

Because of the excitement and energy that the Kitchener, Ontario, project generated, Habitat Canada has made Women Build an annual event.

Habitat in the United States and Canada

Alaska

Canada

Mountain States

Midwest

Northeast

West

ATLANTIC OCEAN

Mid-America

Central Atlantic

Puerto Rico

Middle States

Southeast

Gulf of Mexico

Hawaii

Canada

HFH Canada comprises 52 affiliates in all 10 provinces of Canada, and it has built more than 450 houses throughout the country. In 1993, the Jimmy Carter Work Project took place in Winnipeg, Manitoba, and in Waterloo, Ontario.

HFH Canada faces two main challenges. The first is to educate Canadian citizens about the extent of substandard housing in their communities. Studies have shown that average incomes and the supply of rental housing have declined while rents have increased. However, contrary to the stereotypical ghetto poverty of cities in other countries, Canadian poverty is largely unseen.

The second challenge facing HFH Canada is land acquisition. Despite vast tracts of undeveloped land in the interior, climatic and economic conditions have caused most of the population to settle along the southern border. Land in the urban centers is often too expensive for affiliates, but jobs usually are located in the cities or suburbs, and transportation costs are high.

Yet progress is being made. Volunteers from each province and several American states have attended the annual Ed Schreyer Work Project, an event similar to the Jimmy Carter Work Project honoring former Governor General Ed Schreyer, who is joined by his wife, Lily, on all builds.

HABITAT FACT: Community college and high school students prefabricated walls for the 2000 Ed Schreyer Work Project in Windsor, Ontario.

Central Atlantic

The Central Atlantic region comprises more than 200 affiliates in Maryland, North Carolina, South Carolina, Virginia, Washington, D.C., and West Virginia.

Homeowners partnering with HFH Sea Island in South Carolina, the first affiliate in that state, completed the equivalent of three months of full-time work in sweat equity working on their houses.

Hurricane Floyd provided the Central Atlantic region an opportunity to prove its community-

South Carolina

building skills. Twelve affiliates are working with the Hurricane Floyd Recovery Build Program to help residents of eastern North Carolina rebuild their communities. In addition to working with many communities, partnerships with HFHI, corporate sponsors, other nonprofit organizations, a federal agency, and the city government helped Princeville, North Carolina, the oldest U.S. town chartered by African Americans, rebuild and preserve their history.

The region's goals include improving affiliates' effectiveness in eliminating poverty housing. AmeriCorps VISTA volunteer programs, designed to help organizations increase their capacity to serve, Collegiate Challenge teams, and training, technical support, and challenge grants also have enabled many affiliates to build more houses.

HABITAT FACT: Habitat's ReStores, facilities that sell quality new and used building supplies, are becoming an increasingly important way to raise funds for house building and to protect the environment.

Mid-America

This region comprises about 250 affiliates in Indiana, Kentucky, Ohio, and Tennessee.

As part of Habitat's 25th anniversary, held in Indianapolis, Indiana will build 250 houses in 2001. Addressing poverty in many areas of Appalachia has been a challenge for these states, as well as for some in the Central

Atlantic region. A limited fundraising base and volunteer pool has encouraged affiliates to take advantage of help from outside the area. In 1997, the Jimmy

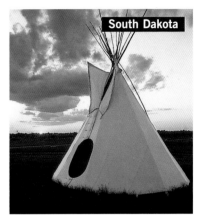

South Dakota

Carter Work Project took place at seven sites scattered throughout eastern Kentucky and Tennessee, resulting in 52 new houses.

For affiliates in the northern part of the region, winter is a time to develop an effective board of directors, update accounting procedures, and plan for upcoming activities. Good cooperation from city and state governments also has contributed to affiliate success here. Some city governments help affiliates acquire affordable land for building. On the state level, legislators have pledged to sponsor Habitat builds in their districts, not only increasing the amount of affordable housing available to low-income residents but also raising awareness of Habitat's mission.

HABITAT FACT: Global Village teams provide funding and labor for several Appalachian affiliates.

New Mexico

Middle States

The Middle States region comprises about 250 affiliates in Arkansas, Kansas, Louisiana, Mississippi, Missouri, Nebraska, Oklahoma, and Texas.

One of the region's special challenges has been to tackle two areas of highly concentrated rural poverty. In the Mississippi Delta, Habitat has seen dynamic activity despite poverty rates that can exceed 30 percent in some areas. In the Rio Grande Valley of south Texas, however, affiliates have had more difficulties making an impact. In part, this reflects the differences in the populations that Habitat serves in each location. Many Delta residents have connections to the area going back generations. By contrast, because of immigration from Mexico, the population in south Texas is much more transitional.

The Middle States region has several rapidly growing cities where buying land is becoming problematic. For regional staff, communication between affiliates is a priority that can help build a regional identity in a geographically diverse region.

HABITAT FACT: One of the components of the Mississippi Delta Initiative's success has been the participation of AmeriCorps VISTA volunteers, who manage volunteer and fundraising programs.

Midwest

The Midwest region comprises 256 affiliates in Illinois, Iowa, Michigan, Minnesota, North Dakota, South Dakota, and Wisconsin.

The Retired and Senior Volunteer Program (RSVP) offers adults age 55 and older opportunities to volunteer at the affiliate level. Participants usually work in groups with responsibilities in board development, family support, fundraising, home repair education, and construction.

In another program, some affiliates are working with tribal communities through Habitat's Native Peoples' Initiative. A lack of resources and opportunities for building in Native communities has led to a tremendous need for affordable housing. The initiative seeks to work with these groups to build environmentally sustainable housing while encouraging posi-tive relationships between Native and non-Native communities.

Both urban and rural areas face similar issues. Opportunities for improvement include increasing access to financial and human resources and combating the sense of community despair that can accompany long-term substandard housing issues. Common strengths include local community residents who care about improving their neighborhoods, donors seeking to target certain areas for renewal, and partnerships with other like-minded organizations.

HABITAT FACT: An Open Door Challenge Fund available in most Midwest region states has helped increase the capacity to build houses through housing grants.

Mountain States

The Mountain States region comprises nearly 160 affiliates in Alaska, Colorado, Idaho, Montana, New Mexico, Oregon, Utah, Washington, and Wyoming.

The Mountain States include many desirable places to live. As a result, land prices are relatively high, presenting Habitat affiliates with one of their biggest challenges. The pressure on land prices is even greater in larger cities and in the many resort areas, resulting in a tremendous need for affordable housing. Poverty is exceptionally high in some smaller communities that once relied on the wood products and mining industries.

Weather conditions in this region vary greatly. In the northern states, the pleasant summer weather attracts church groups and individuals from outside the region, while in the winter months, New Mexico beckons volunteers and RV Care-A-Vanners.

Population centers are more scattered because of the open geography and mountainous terrain. But an annual conference for the Mountain States and West regions has helped to bridge the distance and bring dispersed affiliates together. At this event, affiliates share their expertise on fundraising, legal and financial management, strengthening of faith-community involvement, volunteer program management, and family partnerships.

HABITAT FACT: The affiliate in Fairbanks, Alaska, is the northernmost affiliate in the United States.

Northeast

The Northeast region of Habitat for Humanity is comprised of more than 200 affiliates. The region consists of ten states

Georgia

New York

including Connecticut, Delaware, Maine, Massachusetts, New Hampshire, New Jersey, New York, Pennsylvania, Rhode Island, and Vermont.

Although a majority of the region's affiliates are located in rural areas, many of the United States' largest urban centers are concentrated in this region. Habitat is working aggressively in many large urban centers including Philadelphia, New York, and Boston. As suburbs around these large cities expand, many low-income families are left behind in housing that is aging and decaying. Job opportunities also have moved from the inner cities to the suburbs, putting a strain on social services due to reduced tax income. Furthermore, this population shift has helped make affordable land more difficult to obtain in non-urban areas.

To encourage community redevelopment in the cities, some Habitat affiliates have built in concentrated areas within neighborhoods. Each builder tries to match the historical architectural design of the surrounding area, which means Habitat homes can be anything from rowhouses to rehabilitated condominiums to detached houses. Subsequently, many communities have taken a renewed pride in the area and upgraded infrastructure and built parks and playgrounds.

Campus chapter involvement in the Northeast is high, with nearly 150 active chapters. Many students mentor Habitat home-owners' children and help with fundraising and family-support programs. Some chapters work with others to pool resources in sponsoring houses. Students that participate with Habitat benefit by learning leadership skills and often maintain relationships with local affiliates after they graduate from college.

HABITAT FACT: Several affiliates in the Northeast region have created positions for students on their boards of directors.

Southeast

The Southeast region comprises about 180 affiliates in Alabama, Florida, Georgia, and Puerto Rico. The region's first affiliate, HFH of Collier County (Florida), originally called Immokalee HFH, began in 1978 as one of the four charter Habitat affiliates.

The Southeast's warm weather enables many affiliates to build year-round and attracts volunteers from harsher climates in the winter. However, it has seen its share of tornadoes, hurricanes, and floods. Affiliates have found that building beyond code requirements can help disaster damage.

Rural poverty is a pressing issue. The lack of social services in some areas means that even if a person is highly motivated to improve his or her situation, the limited number of jobs and services can make this goal difficult to

Texas

accomplish. And while land some-times is available for building, there are fewer resources to buy the land, making it as difficult to obtain as in urban areas. But this region has been home to some of Habitat's highest-producing affiliates. Affiliates must manage growth as they increase their house production to ensure healthy relationships with the homeowners and to maintain a ministry focus.

HABITAT FACT: "Snowbirds"—mostly senior citizens who travel to the South for the winter—significantly increase the skilled-volunteer pool for Habitat affiliates.

West

The West region comprises more than 75 affiliates in Arizona, California, Hawaii and Nevada. Tucson Habitat for Humanity, the oldest affiliate in the region, was chartered in 1980.

Several of the issues that many affiliates face throughout the United States are intensified in the West region. The high cost of living, characteristic of many places in the West, is especially problematic in Hawaii, where the transportation costs included in the price of imported consumer goods often make housing unaffordable. However, legislation has made it possible for Native Hawaiians to obtain land and partner with Habitat.

Raising funds to support building in a high-cost region is a challenge, especially in thinly populated areas. Housing costs have escalated to such levels that community development planning is increasingly becoming an issue, and Habitat has the opportunity to advocate affordable housing. Some communities are initially negative about Habitat building in their area, but attitudes usually change when residents learn that their new neighbors may be firefighters, teachers, or police officers.

HABITAT FACT: Some affiliates in California have formed partnerships with local unions to participate in their apprenticeship programs.

Make a World of Difference

Kentucky, U.S.

Georgia, U.S.

California, U.S.

HELP BUILD HOPE

Volunteer and be part of Habitat for Humanity International's campaign to eliminate poverty housing. Whatever your interest, the welcome mat will always be out at one of more than **2,000 affiliates worldwide**. Volunteers swing hammers, serve on committees, raise funds, answer phones, and provide lunches for building crews. Go to Habitat's website for news of special events and builds. Information about some of Habitat's most popular programs is given on the following pages.

HOW YOU CAN HELP: To find your nearest affiliate, log on to www.habitat.org; call (229) 924-6935 (extension 2552); or email your name and address to publicinfo@hfhi.org.

Florida, U.S.

The Philippines

Canada

PARTNER WITH A PRESIDENT

Join former U.S. President Jimmy Carter and his wife, Rosalynn, and thousands of other volunteers for one week each year to raise houses and awareness of the need for affordable housing. The **Jimmy Carter Work Project** builds with families in need, in North America and abroad.

HOW YOU CAN HELP: For more information on how to join a Jimmy Carter Work Project, log on to www2.habitat.org/jcwp or call (229) 924-6935.

California, U.S.

Mexico

Korea

Tennessee, U.S.

Georgia, U.S.

CONSTRUCT A BETTER FUTURE

Work alongside thousands of other students and young people who are helping to eliminate poverty housing. Join a Habitat **Campus Chapter** on a high school or college campus in the United States or in several other countries. If you are too young to build, you can become involved by babysitting, helping with landscaping or fundraising, or joining in other support activities.

HOW YOU CAN HELP: To learn more about Campus Chapters and Youth Programs, log on to www.habitat.org/ccyp/; call (229) 924-6935 (extension 2220); or email campuschapters@hfhi.org.

The Philippines

Papua New Guinea

Northern Ireland

Bolivia

DISCOVER ANOTHER CULTURE

Sign up for a **Global Village** trip—and a world of adventure travel—as you build with families in need around the world. From Kenya to New Zealand to Costa Rica to Korea, participating in a Global Village trip gives you the opportunity to get to know local peoples and their cultures, by living and working side-by-side with them.

HOW YOU CAN HELP: To find out how you can participate, log on to www.habitat.org/GV; call Global Village at (229) 924-6935 (extension 2549); or email gv@hfhi.org.

BUILD A LEGACY

Join a **Women Build** project. Championed by Habitat cofounder Linda Fuller, this innovative program is about including and empowering women, which is only fitting, since many Habitat households are headed by women and half of Habitat's volunteers are women, too. Women Build is active in the United States and around the world.

California, U.S.

HOW YOU CAN HELP: To find out more about Women Build, log on to www.habitat.org/wb; call (229) 924-6935 (extension 2700); or email WomenBuild@hfhi.org.

Ghana

INVOLVE YOUR CHURCH

Suggest that your church form a **Global Faith Partnership** with a church in another part of the world. You can also involve your church and community with Habitat's **International Day of Prayer and Action for Human Habitat,** the third Sunday of September. The day concludes **Building on Faith** week. Volunteers from churches, synagogues, and mosques build houses and hold community-wide worship services, emphasizing Habitat's roots as an ecumenical faith-based ministry.

HOW YOU CAN HELP: Log on to www.habitat.org/cr/; call Habitat's Church Relations department at (800) 365-7990; or email churchrelations@hfhi.org.

Georgia, U.S.

DISCOVER NEW PARTNERSHIPS

Meet people from all walks of life through **RV Care-A-Vanners**, volunteers who travel across North America in their own recreational vehicles, partnering with host affiliates and homeowners to build houses. For many Care-A-Vanners, this work gives them the opportunity to use skills they have honed throughout their lives. When disaster strikes —a hurricane, flood, or earthquake—RV Care-A-Vanners are often among the first to assist other agencies on site.

HOW YOU CAN HELP: To find out more about the RV Care-A-Vanners, call (229) 924-6935 (extension 2446) or email rv_info_desk@hfhi.org.

SUPPORT HABITAT RESTORES AND SAVE

Throughout the United States and Canada, Habitat affiliates have established **ReStores,** which sell high-quality used and surplus building materials for a fraction of retail prices. All the profit goes to construct Habitat houses in the community. By salvaging reusable materials, ReStores also help the environment, diverting tons of usable building supplies from ending up in landfills.

Texas, U.S.

HOW YOU CAN HELP: Log on to www.habitat.org/env/restoreusa.html or call your local affiliate for information about ReStores in your area.

STRENGTHEN TIES WITH NATIVE PEOPLES

Become a part of the **Native Peoples Initiative,** which seeks to increase homeownership for Native Americans, Native Hawaiians, and Native Alaskans. Talk to your tribal government or housing authority about Habitat, start a Habitat affiliate on your reservation, or invite a Habitat representative to your tribal college or tribal meeting. If you live near a reservation, volunteer to help build there.

HOW YOU CAN HELP: For more information, log on to www.habitat.org/npic or call (303) 832-9971.

South Dakota, U.S.

BUILD A BETTER FUTURE

Learn about Habitat's **Prison Partnership** program. Offenders volunteer with Habitat programs set up with correctional facilities. The offenders learn valuable construction skills, which are helpful when they rejoin their communities. At the same time, they help people become homeowners.

HOW YOU CAN HELP: For more information on how your affiliate can become involved in the Prison Partnership program, call (229) 924-6935.

Texas, U.S.

TEAM YOUR EMPLOYER UP WITH HABITAT

Encourage your company to become a **Corporate Sponsor** by donating supplies, giving financial support, or organizing employees to build Habitat houses. House-building strengthens employee teamwork, while Habitat raises a company's profile in the community and can give it a tax deduction.

HOW YOU CAN HELP: For more information, log on to www.habitat.org/cp/; call (229) 924-6935 (extension 2126); or email corp_prog@hfhi.org.

CARE FOR THE ENVIRONMENT

Learn about Habitat's philosophy of sustainable building. Habitat believes in replenishing what it uses, enabling future generations to build healthy homes—and lives. Through the **Environmental Initiative** program, learn how to promote energy-efficient housing and environmentally friendly construction techniques. **The Green Team** helps accomplish these goals through training sessions, newsletters, and bulletins.

HOW YOU CAN HELP: For more information, log on to www.habitat.org.env/; call (229) 924-6935 (extension 2622); or email Const&Env@hfhi.org.

No More Shacks! It Can Happen

THE ELIMINATION OF SUBSTANDARD HOUSING AND HOMELESSNESS is a huge task. But in 25 years, with God's help and the sweat of tens of thousands of volunteers and Habitat homeowners, Habitat for Humanity has been making steady progress. More than a half million people now live in Habitat houses—and we're just getting started!

Habitat for Humanity began with the conviction that everyone needs at least a simple, decent, safe, and healthy place to live. It was started with the belief that every person who desires to help, through working together, can be part of the solution to the problem of substandard housing. It was founded on the assumption that a hand up means more than a handout.

The Habitat model for building houses and hope has remained the same for 25 years: modest but adequate houses built by future homeowners and volunteers working side-by-side; the houses sold to the partner families at no profit, with no interest, and on terms they can afford to pay; and their mortgage payments then used to build more houses with other families desperately in need of shelter. In Habitat for Humanity's home county in south Georgia, that model already has resulted in victory over substandard housing. No one here—no one!—any longer must live in substandard housing. Our 21st Century Challenge—which grew out of the local victory—invites other cities and counties to embrace the goal of eradicating substandard housing in their communities.

Through this work of hammering out faith and love, which has resulted in more than 100,000 houses, we have seen the dramatic difference a decent house makes: Parents, freed from the worry that accompanies inadequate housing, often continue their educations and advance in their jobs; children do better in school; health improves; shaky marriages heal; families get more involved in their churches, their neighborhoods, their communities.

We know from these stories that the Habitat model works. But with more than a billion people worldwide still inadequately sheltered, we know, too, that one model or one group of people cannot answer the profound crisis of substandard housing. Governments must help; more organizations must get involved; more people the world over must become convinced that poverty housing impoverishes us all, and then do something about it. We also know that Habitat for Humanity can and must do more. And, we are committed to doing just that, God being our helper.

Over these past 25 years, I have become firmly convinced that the resources—both human know-how and financial wherewithal—exist to solve this problem. Only the will to do the job is in short supply. With God's help, with hard work, with more and more people accepting the challenge to make a difference, the will to finish the job will evolve and people in every community one day will be able to declare: There are no shameful and hope-robbing shacks or shanties here. We solved that problem…one family at a time.

Millard Fuller, founder and president of Habitat for Humanity International

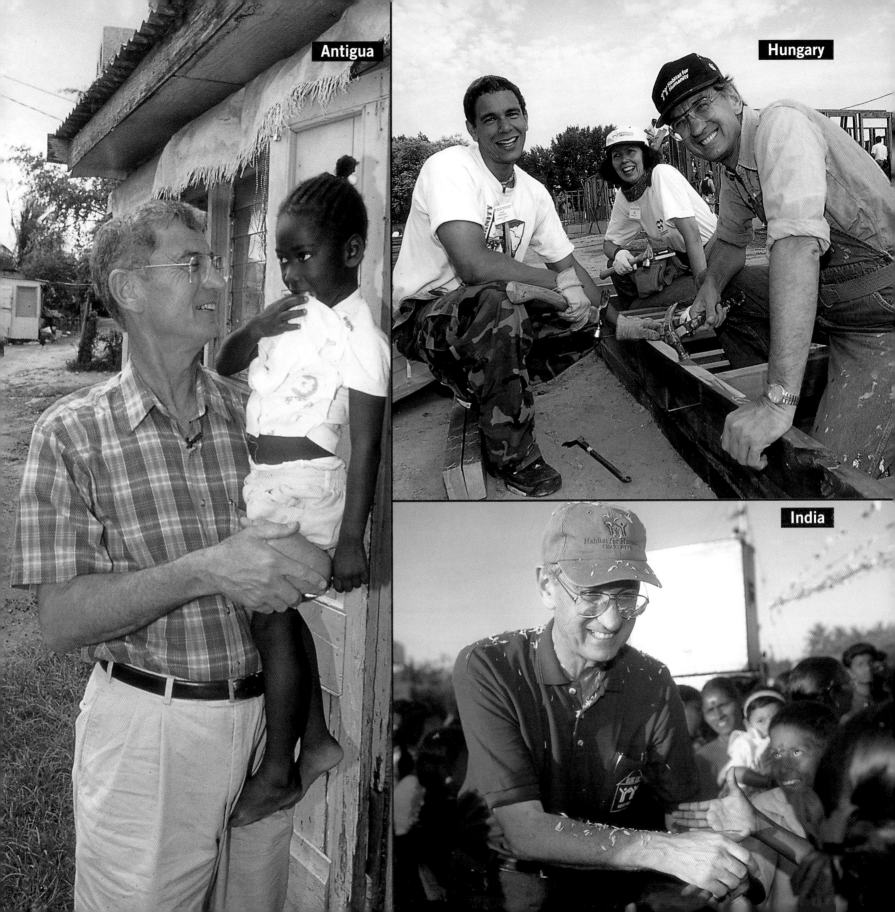

Antigua

Hungary

India

ACKNOWLEDGMENTS

This book could not have been possible without the contributions of many dedicated people who work for Habitat for Humanity International. Habitat's area vice presidents and directors coordinated contributions from affiliates in their area. We would like to thank Harry Goodall (Africa and the Middle East), Steve Weir (Asia and the Pacific), Alane Regualos and Mary Engelking (Europe and the Commonwealth of Independent States), Torre Nelson (Latin America and the Caribbean), and Ted Swisher (United States). Area personnel in Americus, Georgia, were equally helpful: Karan Kennedy (Africa and the Middle East), Nancy Barnes (Asia and the Pacific), John Yeatman (Europe and the Commonwealth of Independent States), Grant Johnson (Latin America and the Caribbean), David Beckerson (Canada), and Kevin Campbell (United States).

From the beginning, Dennis Bender and Jill Claflin in Americus, Georgia, guided the project with clear vision, and Milana McLead gave invaluable guidance and support. Rebekah Graydon's fact checking and proofreading and Angela Murray's photo research came to our rescue many times. Our thanks to the many talented photographers featured here, especially Doral Chenoweth III, Kim MacDonald, and Alysia Peyton.

We'd also like to thank Jennifer Greer and Steve Madden, Anita Mellot in Americus, and Claire Algarme in the Philippines for their help with the text. Scot Ninnemann and the Habitat web site provided invaluable information. Tilly Grey wrote sections on Africa; Milana McLead contributed to Europe and the Philippines; and Steve Little provided the text on El Salvador.

SMALLWOOD & STEWART, New York